Developing study skills

Catherine Littler
Michael Fardon

Published by Osborne Books Limited
Unit 1B Everoak Estate
Bromyard Road, Worcester WR2 5HP
Tel 01905 748071
Email books@osbornebooks.co.uk
Website www.osbornebooks.co.uk

Design by Laura Ingham

Printed by CPI Group (UK) Limited, Croydon, CR0 4YY, on environmentally friendly, acid-free paper from managed forests.

British Library Cataloguing in Publication Data
A catalogue record for this book is available from the British Library

ISBN 978 1909173 545

Contents

Acknowledgements

The publisher wishes to thank the following for their help with the editing, reading and production of the book: Lynne Taylerson, Maz Loton, Bee Pugh and Cathy Turner. Thanks are also due to Laura Ingham for her designs for this series.

The publisher is indebted to the Association of Accounting Technicians for its help and advice to our authors and editors during the preparation of this text.

Authors

Catherine Littler is a Fellow Member of the AAT and a former AAT Coordinator at a major FE training provider. Catherine now works for the AAT as an External Verifier and consultant, supporting new training providers and delivering training to AAT staff and tutors. She is also a lecturer and examiner for the IFS University College on the accounting units for their degree programme.

Michael Fardon has extensive teaching experience of a wide range of banking, business and accountancy courses at Worcester College of Technology. He now specialises in writing business and financial texts and is General Editor at Osborne Books. He is also an educational consultant and has worked extensively in the areas of vocational business curriculum development.

Introduction

what this book covers

This book has been written specifically to cover the Unit 'Developing study skills' which is mandatory for the AAT Level 2 Diploma in Accounting and Business.

The book contains a clear text with illustrative examples and case studies, chapter summaries and key terms to help with revision. Each chapter has a wide range of student activities, many based on the style of the AAT assessment.

Readers should note that Osborne Books has adopted the American spelling 'kinesthetic' to describe one of the three learning styles rather than the UK variant 'kinaesthetic'. This is in order to be consistent with AAT's use of the word 'kinesthetic'.

1 Introduction to study skills

this chapter covers...

This chapter is an introduction to what Study Skills are and how you will learn about them when studying this Unit.

The topics covered in this chapter are:

- *the documents you will have to produce as part of your assessment: a Learning Journal and an Action Plan*

- *a summary of what you will be learning about*

- *how to develop good methods of study*

- *how to plan your time when studying*

- *how to prioritise your areas of study*

- *how to motivate yourself to study effectively*

- *how to manage your time effectively*

- *study tips on how your brain works and how to make the most of the learning opportunities it offers*

WHAT YOU WILL NEED TO PRODUCE IN THIS UNIT

This chapter outlines what you will have to do to complete this Unit and be confident in tackling your assessment. The assessment should take up to twelve weeks to complete.

Learning Journal

One of the main tasks that you will have to do for this Unit is to keep a **Learning Journal**.

A journal is simply a personal record of what you have done and what you think about things. Some people keep a written diary, some people post what they have done and what they think about things on social media sites such as Facebook or Twitter. A Learning Journal is just a special type of journal which you use to write about the methods you use to study and say how your studies are going. It could be described as follows: **a Learning Journal is a record where you write down on a regular basis what you are doing in order to learn.**

You will record:

- the learning activity you did, on what date and what time
- the VAK style of learning you adopt, eg **V**isual (you understand by knowing what something looks like), **A**uditory (you learn by listening to an explanation) and **K**inesthetic (you learn by doing something)
- what notes you have taken, what information you have found and where you got it from
- how you felt about the learning sessions, including any problems you encountered and what you did to solve them

AAT have provided a sample Learning Journal and you may choose to use this format if you wish; an example of one journal entry can be seen below. The Learning Journal will be explained in full in the next chapter.

Learning Journal

Date and time	Learning activity	Learning style (VAK)	Notes taken, resources used, references	Any other comments
9 July 20XX 10.00 - 11.30	Lesson on buyer/seller financial documents. Teacher lecture, then group exercise in document completion.	Visual (saw documents) Auditory (heard teacher's lecture) Kinesthetic (filled in documents).	Notes on lecture, sample documents completed.	Lecture a bit boring but group work using actual documents made it really interesting and easier to understand.

the Learning Journal and your assessment

The Learning Journal will be assessed as part of the Unit so you will have to make sure that you complete it properly throughout the period of study.

You will be asked questions about the Learning Journal and what you have learned from the journal. Your assessor will look at your Learning Journal part way through the Unit and give you feedback. You will also have to mention entries from the journal as evidence so the better the journal, the easier the assessment.

use different note taking techniques

This unit requires you to be able to use several different methods of taking notes. You will have to take notes:

■ during lessons

■ when you are studying on your own, whether at home or in a library

You will find information from sources including books and the internet. You have to know how to find the information and then answer questions about where you obtained the information.

You should be able to direct other people to your sources by using simple **referencing,** including for example:

■ the author and title of a book and date of publication

■ a website address or web page link

You will need to be able to comment on how reliable you think the information is.

plan and present a piece of work using an Action Plan

As well as keeping a Learning Journal you will need to plan and present a set piece of work. This could be a written assignment or a formal presentation. You will need to agree the set piece of work with your assessor and will have to present the work in an appropriate way.

You will have to produce an **Action Plan** as you complete your piece of work.

An Action Plan enables you to organise what you need to do and when you need to do it.

An Action Plan will usually list:

■ a series of tasks to be completed

■ the steps you need to follow to complete the tasks

■ an explanation of how the work will be presented

- the resources you will need for each task – for example textbooks and the internet to research a topic

- the date by which each of the tasks should be completed

- a note made when you have actually completed the task

- notes about problems or delays you have encountered and any changes you have made to the plan including your revised dates

Your assessor will give you feedback on your piece of work and you should use the feedback to improve the work. As part of the assessment, you will have to answer questions on how you improved your work using feedback.

The main headings suggested by the AAT for an Action Plan are shown below. Study the table and the notes that explain the headings. The completion of an Action Plan is explained in full in Chapter 7.

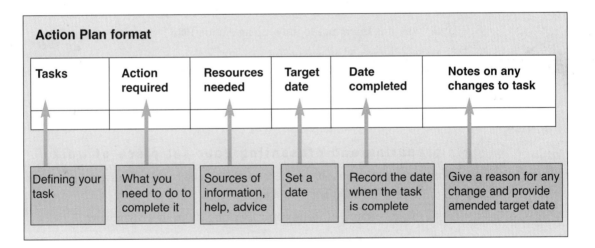

Action Plan format

Tasks	Action required	Resources needed	Target date	Date completed	Notes on any changes to task
Defining your task	What you need to do to complete it	Sources of information, help, advice	Set a date	Record the date when the task is complete	Give a reason for any change and provide amended target date

WHAT YOU ARE GOING TO LEARN IN THIS UNIT – A SUMMARY

Set out below is a summary of what you will need to learn in order to successfully complete your assessment.

you will learn all about the Learning Journal

- how to create a Learning Journal (see page 3)

- how a Learning Journal will help you to understand different ways of studying

- what you should enter into the Learning Journal and what you will learn from the journal

you will learn about the process of learning

■ understanding what **learning styles** are – ie different ways of learning – and how to take advantage of them

■ learning about a wide range of different **learning activities** and whether they involve active learning (learning by doing an activity) or passive learning (eg learning by taking in information, eg reading)

the importance of note taking and organising notes

■ becoming familiar with all the different **sources of information**

■ checking and referencing sources of information

■ becoming familiar with all the different styles of note taking and knowing when to use each of them

planning a set piece of work using an Action Plan

■ why it is important to draw up an Action Plan

■ why Action Plans are useful

■ what an Action Plan should contain

■ amending your Action Plan if you run into problems with your set piece of work

preparing and presenting your set piece of work

■ how to present your set piece of work (which can be delivered in written form or given as a presentation)

■ the importance of using correct writing styles in written work

■ presenting your work confidently to make a good impression

■ using feedback from your tutor to improve your work

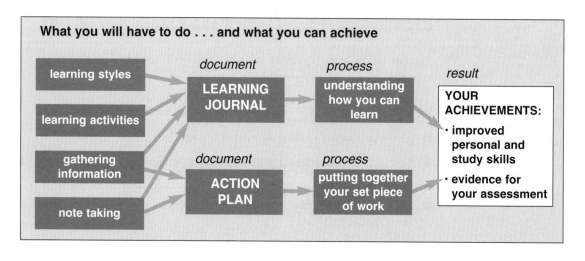

THE BENEFITS OF DEVELOPING GOOD STUDY SKILLS

passing the assessment – the need for study skills

There is no question that the way in which you organise your study makes a huge difference to whether or not you pass your assessment.

Success can depend on what type of student you are and what study skills you are able to develop:

- some students are more comfortable with their learning and find studying for assessments such as exams easier than others – this is quite natural – students who find a course very easy might not do as well on it as others because they might not develop their study skills or do enough work to pass

- students who find the course more of a challenge often work harder and do well; they can also develop a wider range of ways to study – study skills – and will know what helps them to understand the course and how to pass it

Studying in the right way for you will mean that you use your time well. This means that you don't waste your time, don't end up with gaps in your knowledge and are more likely to pass the course. Using a range of study methods makes the learning process more interesting and will help you to remember what you have studied.

Making sure that you can take advantage of all methods and styles of learning means that you will make the most of your ability to learn. If you stick to only the methods and styles you already know about and use and say 'I learn best like this, so that's the only method I will use', you might miss out on valuable and useful new ways to learn and succeed.

In the next Section we will examine what it is that might stop you from studying and we will describe some ways of getting around these barriers.

GETTING STARTED – PLANNING AND MANAGING YOUR TIME

'smart' ways of working

There are a number of excuses that you will often hear people make when they are putting off doing work that they need to do:

'I don't have time.'

Not having time is a common excuse for not doing a piece of work but is it really true? If we are honest with ourselves then we can find enough time.

Another commonly used phrase is:

'If you want something done, ask a busy person.'

Why do you think this phrase is used? Surely if someone is busy then they will not have time to do more work? This phrase is recognising that someone who achieves a lot does so because they **work smart**. These people work hard but do not waste time. They are organised and remember what they need to do.

One of the ways to work smart is to get things done in those 5-10 minute gaps in your day. It is amazing how much can be achieved by just getting on with it when you have a few minutes.

Rather than thinking

'I've got to go out in 10 minutes so I don't have time'

instead ask yourself *'I've got 2 minutes, what can I do?'*

Some people are always busy and get a lot done, others say that they are busy but get little done. Which type of person are you? How do you know?

We will start by examining what you do each week and see what time you really have available.

Set out below is a completed weekly plan for a student who is studying the AAT qualification. Travelling time to and from home to college/work/sports venues has been included in the time allocated to each activity.

Time	Monday	Tuesday	Wednesday	Thursday	Friday	Saturday	Sunday
0800 – 0900							
0900 – 1000	College	College	College				Sports
1000 – 1100							Matches
1100 – 1200							
1200 – 1300							
1300 – 1400							
1400 – 1500					Part time	Part time	
1500 – 1600					Job	Job	
1600 – 1700							
1700 – 1800							
1800 – 1900			Sports				
1900 – 2000			Training				
2000 – 2100							
2100 – 2200							
2200 - 2300							

This student appears to have a lot to do. At college for three days per week and working for two days per week, he or she is probably working a few more hours than is advisable for someone studying full-time. However, there are still plenty of free time slots for relaxation and for home study.

Try drawing up a timetable for yourself, possibly using a spreadsheet.

There is a blank form reproduced on the next page to act as a template which you are free to photocopy, using an enlarging photocopier.

Time	Monday	Tuesday	Wednesday	Thursday	Friday	Saturday	Sunday
0800 – 0900							
0900 – 1000							
1000 – 1100							
1100 – 1200							
1200 – 1300							
1300 – 1400							
1400 – 1500							
1500 – 1600							
1600 – 1700							
1700 – 1800							
1800 – 1900							
1900 – 2000							
2000 – 2100							
2100 – 2200							
2200 - 2300							

Using your own timetable you will be able to see when you have time to study. Allocate some time to studying but keep study sessions short, perhaps hour long sessions, and make sure that there are several sessions spread throughout the week.

doing the right work

We have discussed the need to allocate time and to make good use of those 5-10 minutes in the day when you often just wait for the next activity to start. The other aspect of working smart is to **do the right work**.

We are often told we must work hard but it is equally important to work in the right way on the right tasks to make sure our hard work makes the most impact.

For example, a student needs to be able to answer questions on 5 different topics in an exam. The student must pass all 5 topic areas to pass the exam.

The student likes and is interested in topics 1, 2 and 3 so spends hours and hours working on those areas. The student knows a little bit about topic 4 so then studies that for a few hours. Topic 5 is disliked by the student, as it is difficult to understand. The students puts off studying it, leaving it until the day before the exam. Does that sound familiar?

It is often tempting for students to leave until last the topics that they dislike or find most challenging – or both. It is important, however, to work smart and spend time on the areas of study that are most needed and will have most impact and not put this off.

When you are deciding what to study make sure that you are spending enough time on all topics. Most of all, make sure you spend most time on the topics that you find challenging and currently know least about.

getting started – motivation

So far we have reviewed what you might actually do in a normal week and found that one problem is finding time for difficult areas. The other problem that most people have is that they struggle to actually start working:

'I'll start in a minute'   *'I'll just do this….'*

Then: *'Oh no, that took a bit too long, I haven't got enough time now so I'll do it tomorrow…'*

Studying is about self-discipline. If you, like many people, struggle with forcing yourself to do things that you really do not want to do, here are some suggestions that may motivate you:

- think about how you will feel when you pass

- think about the job you will be able to get when you pass

efficient time management – some suggestions

Here are some specific suggestions about how to organise and manage your study time:

- Break your study period into really small chunks.

  The first chunk may be to say to yourself *'I'll just get my books out'* or *'I'll just switch on my computer'* or perhaps *'I'll just log into the website'*.

  These are not frightening to do and usually get you started.

- If thinking about two hours of study is putting you off, plan to do 15 or 20 minutes instead.

  Short sessions are often more effective than long ones because you are more likely to remember what you did.

- Decide how much work you are going to do rather than how long you will study for – perhaps you can say *'I'll do one example today'*.

- Bribe yourself! Some people call this 'rewards' but whatever you call it, it usually works.

  Note that you may need to bribe/reward your family or partner for leaving you alone to study by spending time with them later.

- It does help to imagine how self-satisfied you will feel when you have done a bit of studying. Then the next time you go to study you can remember that feeling and it will help.

'DID YOU KNOW?' STUDY TIPS

- It is important to understand how your brain works when you study and learn. There are two types of memory: short-term and long-term.

  When you store something in your **short term memory** it is only retained in the brain for a short time. This is useful for things you need to remember today eg '*Don't forget to get some milk on the way home*'.

  When you store something in **long-term memory**, you will retain the information for a much longer time, eg learning to drive a car and learning the Highway Code in order to pass the theory driving test.

- You can use a variety of different study techniques to place information firmly in your long-term memory.

- Research has shown that if you write something down, you are more likely to remember it even if you never read what you have written. This means that you cannot use the excuse '*but I'll never read my notes!*'

- Explaining something to someone makes you understand it better. Your brain has to re-organise the information to explain it and that helps you to understand. So find someone, anyone, to chat to about your studies.

- Students who make sure that they understand and can do everything as they go along put their knowledge and skills into their long term memory. They can spend less time revising for exams and will find later, higher level courses easier.

- If you cram for an exam you may pass by putting information into your short-term memory. That will mean that within a short time you will have forgotten it and will need to relearn it before you can learn more on your next, higher level course. That makes the next courses harder for you.

- Part of your course is about gaining knowledge. The knowledge is tested in the exams but is also needed in later levels of the courses. The best way to make sure that knowledge is in your memory is to regularly test yourself. Make it interesting by using different ways to test yourself and your fellow students.

- The other part of the course is about gaining skills, in other words learning to master techniques like double-entry bookkeeping. The best way to make sure that you are able to do a skill well, whether it is playing sport, playing a musical instrument or learning accountancy skills, is to practise. A lot.

  You need to practise the things that you find hard until they are easy. Then do a bit more.

a final tip – looking after yourself

Scientific research has shown that you can significantly help your studying by looking after yourself properly. Studying when you are tired or hungry is much less effective, but many students ignore this advice and do not get enough sleep and do not eat before class. If you do not look after yourself then you are greatly reducing your ability to learn.

This means that you should:

■ **get enough sleep** – plan to sleep for 8 hours a night, every night

■ **eat** properly and regularly and healthily - especially at breakfast time

■ **exercise regularly** – for example going for a daily walk or to the gym

Walking and talking with a friend, discussing your studies, is a really effective way of learning.

Chapter Summary

■ To complete this Unit you will have to keep a Learning Journal and answer questions about what you have learned from your Learning Journal.

■ You will have to complete and present a set piece of work using an Action Plan. The Action Plan will be assessed and you will have to answer questions about the Action Plan.

■ You will have to demonstrate at least two different note taking techniques for the assessment.

■ Good students sometimes fail because of poor study techniques and less confident students often pass because of good study techniques.

■ You can find time to study.

■ It is important to spend time on the right topics when studying.

■ It is important to test your knowledge regularly.

■ It is important to practise skills like double-entry regularly.

■ Learning as you go through the course is more effective than cramming for exams.

■ Getting started is difficult, but you can do it.

■ A task started is a task half-way to completion.

■ You need to get enough sleep, food and exercise to make the most of your learning.

Key Terms		
	study skills	the skills that you acquire which enable you to learn effectively
	short-term memory	the part of your brain which receives information and stores it temporarily before passing it into long-term memory or discarding it
	long-term memory	the ability to retain information and remember processes and concepts for the long-term – useful for effective learning
	VAK	Learning classified as: **V**isual – you learn from what you see **A**uditory – you learn from what you hear **K**inesthetic – you learn by doing something
	Learning Journal	a record where you write down on a regular basis what you are doing in order to learn
	Action Plan	a document which enables you to organise tasks that you need to complete and sets deadlines for their completion
	set piece of work	the basis of your assessment – it can take the form of a written set of tasks or a presentation

Activities

Tick the correct answers for each question.

Note that there may be more than one correct answer to a question.

1.1 You need to record every study session in your Learning Journal because (tick the correct options):

		✔
(a)	The journal itself will be assessed	
(b)	You will have to answer questions about what you have learned by keeping your Learning Journal during your studies	
(c)	You need to be able to talk about entries in your Learning Journal in your assessment	

1.2 What is the minimum number of different note taking techniques that you have to demonstrate in your assessment?

		✔
(a)	1	
(b)	2	
(c)	3	
(d)	4	

1.3 What is the minimum time for a study session?

		✔
(a)	2 minutes	
(b)	10 minutes	
(c)	30 minutes	
(d)	45 minutes	

1.4 On which one of these topics should you spend more of your study time? ✔

(a)	A topic that you find easy and enjoy	
(b)	A topic that you find hard even though you usually get the correct answers to the questions	
(c)	A topic that you find hard and don't get correct	

1.5 Does talking about what you are studying make any difference to how well you understand or remember the information? ✔

(a)	Yes, it helps the brain organise and sort information	
(b)	No, it just bores the listener	

1.6 Knowledge and Skills are terms which mean the same thing. ✔

(a)	True	
(b)	False	

1.7 What are the benefits of using a variety of different study techniques? ✔

(a)	It makes learning more interesting	
(b)	It helps you to put information in your long-term memory	
(c)	None, because it is important to rely on only one study technique	

1.8 Regular exercise helps your learning processes. ✔

(a)	True	
(b)	False	

2 Creating the Learning Journal

this chapter covers...

This chapter explains how to set up the Learning Journal in which you will need to record your learning for this Unit.

You will learn in this chapter:

■ *that keeping a Learning Journal is a way of collecting information on how you learn so that you can improve your ability to learn*

■ *that the information you put into your journal is important for your studies*

■ *that there are different ways of setting out a Learning Journal*

■ *how to lay out your journal in columns*

■ *what the columns are for*

■ *the types of entries made in the Learning Journal – for example experimenting with different learning activities and learning styles*

■ *the importance of reflecting on your methods of learning and developing the methods which best help you learn*

■ *that information from your Learning Journal will be used as evidence in your assessment*

■ *that this book uses the AAT recommended layout for a Learning Journal*

WHY YOU NEED TO KEEP A LEARNING JOURNAL

learning to learn

In your time at school or college you may well have developed ideas about the best ways to learn. This '**learning to learn**' is an important life skill. If you can develop this skill in your studying you will benefit by:

■ finding learning easier

■ continually increasing your knowledge and skills, and importantly . . .

■ increasing your earning potential now and in the future

A **Learning Journal** enables you to do this. But it is useful in the first place to know what exactly a 'journal' is.

what is a journal?

A journal is a place for gathering information. Examples of 'journals' include local newspapers, personal diaries, blogs, Facebook comments, tweets, records of entries in an accounting system. The list is very long. It is useful to think about what a basic 'journal' actually is and does. Internet search engines will tell you that it is:

'a daily record of news and events of a personal nature'

'a personal record of occurrences, experiences, and reflections kept on a regular basis'

what is a Learning Journal?

As we saw in the last chapter, a **Learning Journal** is a specialised journal which concentrates on your methods of study and your assessment of how your studies are getting on. It could be defined as follows: **a Learning Journal is a record where you write down on a regular basis what you are doing in order to learn.**

If we look again at the search engine definitions of 'Learning Journal' quoted above, we will see that the important features are:

■ a learning activity is given a date and time

■ the learning activity is described – it is a 'record'

■ the learning activity affects you as a person – it is 'personal'

■ you can 'reflect' and make comments on the activity

AAT have provided a sample Learning Journal and you may choose to use this format if you wish; an example of a journal entry can be seen on the next page. The entries are described in more detail in the boxes below the journal.

Learning Journal – sample entry

Date and time	Learning activity	Learning style (VAK)	Notes taken, resources used, references	Any other comments
9 July 20XX 10.00 - 11.30	Lesson on buyer/seller financial documents. Teacher lecture, then group exercise in document completion.	Visual (read documents) Auditory (heard teacher's lecture) Kinesthetic (filled in documents).	Notes on lecture, handouts given, sample documents completed.	Lecture a bit boring (a lot of listening and reading handouts) but the group work filling in documents and role play made it much easier to learn the topic.
the date and time – both are important details for analysing patterns of learning	Here you state the **topic covered** and what different **types of learning** you experienced, eg sitting, listening and writing notes and active learning (working with others)	These are the **learning styles** (ways of learning) you experience: **Visual** (looking) **Auditory** (listening) **Kinesthetic** (doing) – known by their initials: **VAK**	Here you state what notes you took or what handouts you were given. You will need to state where they came from (ie give their references)	Here you record what you felt about the activity, what you learned and why the learning was successful – or unsuccessful. You should also record what you did not understand

THE JOURNAL HELPING YOU UNDERSTAND YOUR LEARNING

what is a good Learning Journal?

A good Learning Journal will show you what you are actually doing and what you think about each activity. This journal will not simply be about describing past events, you will make experimental changes to the way that you learn to see if they work. You will do this by looking at a number of entries and thinking about what happened. Then trying to do things differently.

how to make a good Learning Journal

It is likely that looking back over the Learning Journal you will be surprised about what you enjoyed, what helped you learn and how effective some of your changes actually were.

What you will learn from the Learning Journal will depend on several things:

- how clearly you lay out the journal (to make it easier to complete)

- how much detail you put into the entries in the journal

■ resisting the temptation to fill in the journal at the end of the day or at the end of the week – fill it in straight after each period of study

■ making frequent and accurate entries into the journal, the more accurate the data available, the better the journal

■ being honest and recording a true reflection about how you felt during the period of study – this will enable you to get the most benefit from your work

When you have completed a number of entries which have involved different learning methods, you will be able to identify what you find challenging and what really does go well. You can then try to change the way you interact in a lesson or change something about your method of home study to see if these changes help. In this way the journal will help you to decide if your experimental changes work.

a note on passive and active learning

We have already seen that there are three basic learning styles recorded in the Learning Journal: Visual, Auditory and Kinesthetic (VAK styles).

Another classification of learning style contrasts:

■ **passive learning**, where the student simply listens to a lecture or repeats routine calculations without thinking, calculating VAT for example

■ **active learning**, on the other hand is where the student takes responsibility for the learning process and actively questions, discusses or engages in group discussions, quizzes and role play, or works through real-life business situation questions to obtain figures for carrying out financial calculations

Studies have shown that active learning is more effective in enabling students to retain information. This topic is covered in full in the next chapter.

extended example of a Learning Journal

On the next page is set out a complete Learning Journal covering the work undertaken by Marco Allievo, a Level 2 Accounting and Business student over a day and a half. Read through each activity, noting

■ the timing of the activity – learning at college or at home

■ the nature of the learning activity – active or passive, individual or group

■ the learning style – Visual, Auditory or Kinesthetic (VAK)

■ the proportion of resources used which relate to active learning

■ comments which indicate successful learning and unsuccessful learning, areas of difficulty and what was done to overcome them

Learning Journal of a student, Marco Allievo				
Date and time	Learning activity	Learning style (VAK)	Notes taken, resources, references	Any other comments
29 Sept 14.00-15.00	Lecture about control accounts. Classroom-based, passive learning.	VA	Slides handed out by Mr Ali.	It was quite easy – it all made sense.
1 Oct 9.00-9.45	Control accounts – practice examples. Classroom-based, active learning. Individual work.	VK	Handout 'Double-entry 5' and Mr Ali's lecture slides from 29 Sept.	I couldn't remember anything from the lecture on 29 Sept! I had to keep looking at the slides. I wish I had made notes on the slides as I had to ask a lot of questions today. I made mistakes balancing accounts which affected the trial balances so I need to practise balancing accounts.
1 Oct 10.00-11.30	Letter writing – layout, format and type of language in a business letter. Classroom based in computer room. Group work and individual work. Some passive and some active learning.	VAK	Handout 'Writing Business letters' by Miss Boyd.	At the beginning I didn't know what to write but I am starting to get the hang of it. I found group discussions about what to put into the letter to be really helpful. Still don't like writing - I need more practice and more help to feel confident.
1 Oct 12.30-14.30	Sales documentation – sorting and matching documents. Invoice calculations. Classroom based active learning, pair work and individual work.	VK	We used documents in pairs which were handed back in at the end of the lesson. Invoice calculations were done onto pre-printed forms which we kept.	This activity helped me to see how important it is to carefully check the documents – I didn't notice that company A had received 3 instead of 4 items. Invoice calculations are easy, I remembered how to do them without any problem.
1 Oct 18.00-18.30	Practice balancing accounts. Home Study, active learning, individual work.	VK	Used the work from this morning, balancing off and copying T accounts.	I checked the answers against the correct answers that I wrote down this morning. Got the first couple wrong then suddenly it clicked!

Journal completion – avoiding negative comments

You can see from the entries on the previous page that most of the columns are straightforward to complete. Make sure that you complete the columns with enough detail to get maximum information from the journal. The next section in this chapter discusses what information you need to get from your journal. Your journal entries should be about yourself and your learning and should not comment on other people except to say, for example:

> *'I found it useful when Mary explained how to calculate VAT.'*

> *'Mr Ali's diagram made it easier to understand how invoices are sent from one business to another.'*

These examples will help you to identify how useful auditory (Mary's) or visual (Mr Ali's) learning methods are for your learning. Your journal should never be negative and comment on other people's faults, for example:

> *'My teacher is so boring and has his favourites in the class.'*

WHAT INFORMATION WILL I NEED FROM MY JOURNAL?

Your journal will provide you with two main areas of information:

- it will help you to understand how you as an individual learn best; it will also help you improve your skills in working with learning styles which are not necessarily your preferred learning styles

- your assessment – you will need information and evidence from the journal to answer questions in your assessment, and in addition the journal itself will also be assessed

These two main areas of information are explained below.

reflection on your learning

Reading through the journal entries on the previous page, you will see that Marco was quite happy with the lecture on control accounts and did not feel the need to take any notes. However in the next lesson he realised that he could not remember much. That has happened to all of us at some time.

What Marco needs to pick up from the Journal is whether or not this is a regular occurrence. It may be that while he enjoys and understands lectures, he tends not to remember what was said. If that pattern is recognised then it becomes very clear that a lecture, where there is a lot of listening, is not always the best way for him to learn, even though he may enjoy the lecture.

Marco will have to take ownership of his learning by **reflecting on** and **developing** his methods of learning. He should try to develop a method for remembering what is covered in lectures as this will mean he will get more from them and can then perform better in his assessment. This is where the experimenting comes in.

experimentation with study methods

Suppose the student goes to the next lecture and tries to write down as much as possible. How does that work? It might work or it might not work. The student might conclude that he has missed parts of the lecture because he spends all his time scribbling away and not identifying the main points and summarising them. Other possible options for improving learning in this situation could include:

- making use of any handouts/slides in a lesson and developing the information on the slides with notes on what the lecturer is saying

- learning to identify the main points being made and summarising them in your own words rather than trying to repeat the words of the lecturer

- re-writing your notes after the lecture to make sure that the notes make sense for later revision

- downloading lecture slides/notes and comparing them with your notes and those of other students, asking other students or the lecturer about any areas that need clarification

Note that all these alternatives are **active learning** – where you have to think about what is being said and ask questions – rather than sitting back and **passively** listening to the lecture.

The journal can then be used to compare changes in learning techniques with actual results achieved by the student. The reviewing of results against experimental changes to study methods is known as **evidence based experimentation**.

the Learning Journal and your Assessment

For the purposes of the assessment you will need to provide evidence from your Learning Journal. You will need to:

- provide a completed Learning Journal done over at least six weeks

- identify your own preferred learning style, giving reasons why it is your preferred style and using examples from the journal as evidence

- identify when you have used different note taking techniques, using evidence from the journal as well as the notes themselves

- identify when you have worked with other people and what you did, noting what was good or not so good about working with others

- identify when you have found and used information and describe in your journal how you checked that the information was valid

ALTERNATIVE FORMATS FOR THE LEARNING JOURNAL

So far in this book we have used the AAT five column sample format for the Learning Journal because it contains all the headings that you will need.

But there is nothing to say that you cannot amend this format if you want to. Perhaps you may find that it does not give you enough room or flexibility to record what you need. You may find, for example, that you need more than five columns. If you use a spreadsheet for the journal, adding columns is an easy operation.

Here are some examples of possible split columns:

1 Split the 'Date and Time' column into separate **Date** and **Time** columns for clarity.

2 Split the 'Learning Activity' column into two separate columns:

– **Learning Activity: what I did** (eg learning about financial documents)

– **Learning Activity: type of learning** (college or home study, individual, pair or group work)

3 Split the 'Any other comments' column into **types of comment**, eg negative or positive feedback.

These 3 splits are illustrated and explained in the Learning Journal below.

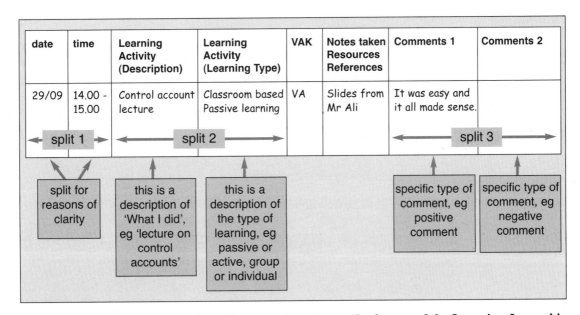

date	time	Learning Activity (Description)	Learning Activity (Learning Type)	VAK	Notes taken Resources References	Comments 1	Comments 2
29/09	14.00 - 15.00	Control account lecture	Classroom based Passive learning	VA	Slides from Mr Ali	It was easy and it all made sense.	

split 1 — split for reasons of clarity

split 2 — this is a description of 'What I did', eg 'lecture on control accounts' / this is a description of the type of learning, eg passive or active, group or individual

split 3 — specific type of comment, eg positive comment / specific type of comment, eg negative comment

The important thing to remember if you want to change the format of the Learning Journal is that the revised format will need to be approved by your assessor before you start using it.

Chapter Summary

- People sometimes think that there are only limited methods of learning about a subject and that you are either good at learning or you are not. This is a false assumption – there are many different ways of learning.

- A Learning Journal is a personal diary which records the different ways in which you learn, what you did and how successful you thought each of the learning methods were.

- The AAT has set out a sample Learning Journal with five column headings but you can add to them or split a column into more than one column. This could make it easier for you to make sure that you include everything that you need.

- You must agree your Learning Journal layout with your assessor before you start using the journal.

- To keep the journal accurate, it should be completed after each study session.

- Your journal will record what you honestly felt about each study session.

- Your journal is about your work and should not comment on teachers and other students.

- You will use the journal to find out what works and what does not work for you.

- You will then use the journal to record experimental changes to your study methods, to judge the success of those changes and possibly then make changes to your learning methods.

- You will need information and evidence from your journal to pass your assessment.

Key Terms		
	Learning Journal	a record or diary where you write down on a regular basis what you are doing in order to learn
	learning activity	the topic covered and the types of learning used, ie active or passive, group or individual, home or college based
	learning style (VAK)	three different processes used to take in information: Visual – you learn from what you see Auditory – you learn from what you hear Kinesthetic – you learn by doing something
	passive learning	you learn by watching and listening to others, such as your teacher, rather than by doing activities yourself
	active learning	a learning process where you learn by actively questioning and thinking about the topic, engaging the brain to problem solve or to link to earlier learning
	reflection on learning	the process of reviewing your methods of learning and adopting methods which produce the best results
	evidence based experimentation	the reviewing of results of experimental changes to study methods

Activities

Tick the correct answers for each question.

Note that there may be more than one correct answer to a question.

2.1 'Learning to learn' is an important skill for you to develop because: ✔

(a)	It will help you progress in your career if you are good at learning	
(b)	Your main aim is to pass all your exams	
(c)	It makes it easier for you to learn, and will enable you to enjoy your learning	
(d)	The more you learn properly, the more you will be able to learn	

2.2 The Learning Journal is: ✔

(a)	An educational magazine	
(b)	A record of your learning activities	
(c)	A way of learning about what methods of learning suit you	
(d)	A way of learning how to improve your learning methods	

2.3 What you are able to learn from your Learning Journal will depend on you: ✔

(a)	Making entries after every study session	
(b)	Recording what your friends think	
(c)	Completing the journal accurately	
(d)	Recording your thoughts honestly	
(e)	Making entries that will make your teacher feel happy	

2.4   Headings in your Learning Journal will include: ✔

(a)	Lecturer's Name	
(b)	Learning Area	
(c)	Learning Activity	
(d)	Learning Style	

2.5   Look at the following three entries into the 'Any Other Comments' column and tick the most appropriate Learning Journal entry.   ✔

(a)	'I hate double-entry'	
(b)	'I had difficulty with double-entry: I understand that I need to debit the bank to put money in and credit the bank to take money out, but I don't really understand the difference between expenses and liabilities.'	
(c)	'I had difficulty with double-entry. Another student kept asking questions, so I couldn't think straight.'	

2.6   To help you to develop and improve your learning you can use the Learning Journal to:

✔

(a)	Identify which learning styles work well and which are poor learning styles for you	
(b)	Record experiments in which you use different learning methods	
(c)	Keep a record of which subjects you don't like and avoid them	

2.7   What will you need from your Learning Journal to pass the assessment?   ✔

(a)	I will simply have to do my journal	
(b)	I will have to answer questions about my journal but if I get stuck I should make a reasonable guess at the right answers	
(c)	I will need to write about things that are recorded in my journal, identifying entries in my journal as evidence	

3 Learning styles

this chapter covers...

This chapter will expand and develop your understanding of the learning styles, eg VAK, passive and active learning, which have been introduced in the last two chapters:

■ VAK, meaning Visual, Auditory and Kinesthetic, are styles of learning which describe the different ways in which you prefer to receive and process information

■ different learners learn better in different ways

■ you will discover that you have some control over how you receive and process information in every learning situation

■ your Learning Journal will be used to identify which learning style(s) suit you best

■ some learning is 'active' and some is 'passive'

■ there are some types of information or topics that are suitable for passive learning, but there are major advantages to actively engaging in learning

■ you can change passive learning situations into active learning sessions

■ moving information from your short-term memory to your long-term memory is key to long term learning success

■ learning is not simply about passing your next exam, it is about making it easier to succeed in all your exams at all levels

■ it is important that it is **you** who maintains control over your learning

WHAT IS YOUR BEST METHOD OF LEARNING?

'What is your best method of learning?'

This is not as straightforward a question as you might think. Most people will be able to state what type of learning they like and what type of learning situation or style that they dislike or feel is difficult.

But what you think is your best method may not be your most effective way of learning. You might feel that you like to learn by sitting back and listening to a teacher or watching a video, but then you will find that while you like these forms of learning, actually you discover that you learn better in a different way.

This is where the Learning Journal becomes so important. By experimenting with different types and styles of learning and then evaluating how successful they are in terms of your ability to absorb and memorise the learning, you can find out what your 'best' method is.

As we saw in the last chapter, you should experiment by changing the way you study and then review the results to see if you are more successful – this is called **evidence-based experimentation**.

By doing this, you will have proved scientifically that 'what I like doing' may not be the same as 'what I do best'.

We will now describe in more detail the learning styles that form an important part of the Learning Journal.

LEARNING STYLES

The AAT has chosen **VAK** as a useful set of learning styles which you can experiment with during your course. The idea behind VAK is that different people like to receive and process information in different ways.

The VAK learning styles are:

■ **V**isual input – where you see or read

■ **A**uditory input – where you hear

■ **K**inesthetic – where you do activities such as puzzles or making things

You can use a **diagnostic test** to find out which learning style or styles will work best for you and there are a number of free tests available online.

To give you an idea of which learning style suits you best try entering 'VAK tests' in an online search engine. The results you get will enable you to identify your 'best' method of learning and also your least effective learning method.

the type of questions found in a VAK test

Set out in the table below are the type of questions you might find in a VAK test. Try counting up the number of answers that are appropriate to you in each column and recording and comparing the totals. You may find that you want to give more than one answer for each situation; this does not matter at all – what you are doing in this case is combining your VAK styles.

situation:	what would be your answer in these situations?		
	visual	**auditory**	**kinesthetic**
when I revise for an exam, I . . .	read all my revision notes	get a 'study buddy' to explain a concept	write out summaries of my notes
I spend my free time	watching movies	chatting on my mobile	texting
When I remember a friend, I . . .	see his/her face	hear his/her voice	think about what we did together
I need to operate a new DVD player	I read the instructions	I ask someone for an explanation	I have a go and learn as I go along
when I get lost in the city centre	I look at a map	I find someone to tell me the way	I walk around until I recognise where I am
	YOUR TOTAL?	*YOUR TOTAL?*	*YOUR TOTAL?*

Doing this VAK test will help in a number of ways:

- it will give you a better idea of what is meant by Visual, Auditory and Kinesthetic learning styles

- it will give you an initial idea of which VAK style is best for you

- it will show you that you may well use a mix of VAK styles

- by finding out which styles you prefer least at the moment, you can see which ones you can experiment with and develop your use of them

- you will eventually be able to complete your Learning Journal accurately

We will now describe the three VAK learning styles in more detail.

visual input – the digital revolution

Recently we have had an immense increase of visual input into our lives. Televisions, computers and an increasing number of portable devices mean that we can have information about almost anything given to us easily in visual form anywhere and most of the time.

At work, computers have become smarter and faster and are used nearly everywhere. In education, we see visual learning used widely in elearning and through the use of interactive smart boards and projectors in the classroom.

visual input and learning

Visual learning is where we learn by seeing.

Students enjoy (or like to use) and are stimulated by all the different types of visual input. Often when we use a visual resource, it is also mixed with auditory input, for example a video which has sound. Visual input can also be mixed with kinesthetic input, for example a picture puzzle or video game.

Here are some examples of **solely** visual input used in the learning process:

- reading a textbook

- looking at handouts

- looking at diagrams and illustrations

- watching a slide presentation without sound

auditory input

Auditory input is about learning through hearing.

Do you like to hear an explanation when studying?

Here are some examples of auditory input you might experience:

- listening to a lecture
- listening to a podcast
- listening to a spoken explanation

It was once thought that with so much visual equipment available that auditory activities would go out of fashion. But trainee professionals such as accountants find them very useful as they can listen to audio resources such as podcasts while walking or travelling on the train and use them as part of their workplace training.

Trainees can also revise material by listening to recordings of lectures by their trainer – with their trainer's permission – when they are at home.

When deciding if you prefer an auditory style, you should ask yourself:

■ how much do you learn and remember from hearing it?

■ what can you do to help yourself learn when you hear new material?

These can both be answered through the writing and analysis of a personal Learning Journal.

kinesthetic learning

Kinesthetic learning is where you actively engage in a task in order to learn.

This type of learning is often linked to 'hands on' subjects like catering or mechanics. Actually, a lot of learning is done kinesthetically in all subjects, even academic ones like accountancy where practising tasks is a very useful learning process. It is well known that many students studying accountancy can only learn double-entry bookkeeping by doing it.

Learning a skill is about practising to get better at that skill.

Here are some examples of kinesthetic learning:

■ practising examples, eg balancing double-entry accounts

■ taking part in a group or team activity

■ interactive e-learning

■ quizzes and puzzles

■ crosswords

combining VAK learning styles

As you will have seen when looking at the sample VAK test earlier in the chapter, you are likely to use a combination of all three learning styles rather than just concentrating on one.

If you look back at the completed Learning Journal in Chapter 2 (page 22), you will see that every activity example involves two or three methods of input, usually Visual with one or both of Auditory and Kinesthetic.

It is important to understand that just because a classroom session or study activity seemed easy and enjoyable, you may not have learned from it as much as you thought at the time.

This is shown in the example on the next page.

what style suits me best?

Look below at the first entry in the example Learning Journal illustrated in Chapter 2. The student has written about a lecture on control accounts which had both visual and auditory input from the trainer:

Learning Journal of a student, Marco Allievo (extract)				
Date and time	**Learning activity**	**Learning style (VAK)**	**Notes taken, resources, references**	**Any other comments**
29 Sept 14.00-15.00	Lecture about control accounts. Classroom-based, passive learning.	VA	Slides handed out by Mr Ali.	It was quite easy - it all made sense.
1 Oct 9.00-9.45	Control accounts – practice examples. Classroom-based, active learning. Individual work.	VK	Handout 'Double-entry 5' and Mr Ali's lecture slides from 29 Sept.	I couldn't remember anything from the lecture on 29 Sept! I had to keep looking at the slides. I wish I had made notes on the slides as I had to ask a lot of questions today.

The 'Any other comments' column entry for 29 September says:

'It was quite easy - it all made sense.'

The next session with Mr Ali was the following day and it had both visual and kinesthetic activities and resources. The comment about this was:

'I couldn't remember anything from the lecture on 29 Sept! I had to keep looking at the slides. I wish I had made notes on the slides as I had to ask a lot of questions today.'

You could decide after reading this journal that the learning style used in the lecture on the 29th was not the most useful one for the student because he did not remember the material from it two days later. This might mean that he does not learn best when information is given using a combination of visual and auditory methods.

This is something that Marco should work on because being able to listen to, understand and remember explanations is a learning activity that occurs very often. He will not be able to avoid listening to a lecturer even if it is – for him – a less effective learning method. Fortunately he has identified a potential solution to the problem. He suggests that taking notes on the lecture slides might help in future.

He will also have to experiment to find ways to make listening to lectures work for him. You will learn more about this in a section called 'taking control of your learning' later in this chapter (pages 39-41).

ACTIVE AND PASSIVE LEARNING

short-term and long-term memory – a revision note

Before learning about active and passive learning it will be useful to remind yourself about the difference between short-term memory and long-term memory discussed in Chapter 1:

- in **short-term memory**, information is only retained for a limited time, eg *'Don't forget to buy some milk for the weekend.'*

- **long-term memory** retains information for a much longer period of time, eg learning to drive a car and learning the Highway Code in order to pass the theory driving test

These concepts will be explained in more depth at the end of this chapter.

ways of learning

Learning is not simply about whether you prefer to 'see', 'hear' or 'do' (the VAK styles of learning). It is also about the methods or activities that you use. It is particularly about the way you personally take part in the learning process. So what kind of learning is active or passive?

passive learning

Passive learning is a traditional form of learning where a person learns by memorising something or by doing as asked without asking many questions. For example:

- listening to a lecture

- re-doing the same thing over and over again, eg learning your multiplication tables 'by rote' – this means saying them again and again and again and again until they remain in your long-term memory

- repeating a calculation again and again until it remains in your long-term memory

active learning

Active learning may be a better way of making sure that facts and ideas are retained in long-term memory. By using active learning, information is not just listened to and noted down during a lecture, it is experimented with and used with a variety of activities which make it more memorable.

Active learning is about using and applying the new ideas you have gained and about linking them to what you already know to build better, more detailed knowledge.

A student who engages in active learning is likely to learn more quickly and show better understanding at a higher level. Examples of active learning are:

■ questioning why and what next?

■ checking your understanding

■ working with case studies and real examples from the workplace to link them to what you already know

Active learning asks you to think about new ideas and to try to work out answers for yourself. An active learner will always ask 'why?' rather like a young child who learns by experimentation and questioning – watching others and working out how to do everything by trying again and again, and asking lots of questions such as 'Why? How? What next?'

The example below shows the learning methods used in dealing with VAT calculations.

Example:

passive and active learning – VAT calculations

tasks

You have been asked to carry out two VAT calculations:

1   A customer is being charged £50 for some goods and VAT has to be added to this amount. What is the amount that the customer will have to pay?

2   A supplier sends a receipt for £60 including VAT, but the VAT amount has not been shown separately on the document, just the £60. What is the VAT amount that has been included in the £60?

answer to calculation 1 – using passive learning

You are likely to use a variety of calculation methods which you could have learned **passively** by rote:

(a) Enter the net figure of £50 into your calculator and press the correct buttons to calculate 20% of £50, ie:

50 x 20 % = £10

(b) If you understand percentages, knowing that 'per cent' means 'out of 100' then you would enter:

50 ÷ 100 x 20 = £10

Either way you will get the correct answer of £10. You have used **passive** (by rote) learning to obtain this answer.

answer to calculation 2 – using passive and active learning

A supplier has given you a receipt for £60 including VAT at 20% but the VAT amount has not been shown separately. You have been taught that all you need to do to find this amount is to divide the gross amount of £60 by 6, which in this case gives a VAT total of £10.

This answer has been reached using **passive** learning: all you need to remember is to divide the gross amount by 6. You have no idea how the number 6 has been arrived at.

Active learners may not be happy with this 'divide the total by 6' rule. Where does the number 6 come from? What if the VAT rate changes? Will the rule still work? The answer is 'no'. The active learner then asks 'Why?' and 'How?'

If you then wanted a formula for this calculation which you could apply to **any** VAT rate, the teacher is likely to give you the following:

$$\frac{\text{VAT rate (\%)}}{\text{100\% + VAT rate (\%)}} \quad \text{x total amount (£)} \quad = \quad \text{VAT content (£)}$$

So applying this formula to the £60 receipt with unknown VAT at 20% you get:

$$\frac{20\%}{120\%} \quad \text{x} \quad £60 \quad = \quad £10 \text{ VAT content}$$

Your teacher then points out that the fraction 20/120 can be reduced to 1/6 by dividing the figures by 20, and that is where the 'dividing by 6' comes from.

You then ask what would happen if VAT was increased to 25%. The formula can be used for this (or any) figure as well:

$$\frac{25\%}{125\%} \quad \text{x} \quad £60 \quad = \quad £12 \text{ VAT content}$$

The teacher asks for the figure you could use for 25% VAT, instead of the six for 20%. The solution is to reduce the 25/125 fraction by dividing both figures by 25 (the top number).

The answer is 1/5, so you need to divide the £60 by 5, giving a result of £12

active learners have deeper knowledge

Students who used the active learning methods in the examples above have a deeper knowledge of VAT calculations because they have developed methods for completing calculations which will work with a range of percentage problems, not just this VAT example.

The passive learners will get the correct answer this time using the 'divide by 6 rule' but won't be able to use this rule if the VAT rate changes or be able to apply it to a different percentage calculation question, such as a corporation tax problem.

The active learner seeks to fully understand principles behind the calculation and will be more able to:

■ use active learning methods again in a different situation when needed

■ understand and complete a wide range of percentage-based calculations at this level in other units

■ progress more easily onto higher level units with more complex calculations

■ impress employers by having a better understanding of the calculations used in the workplace

how to succeed in active learning – some tips

Learning to learn actively can be hard to start with but it does become easier over time. It becomes a habit which is enjoyable, but do remember the following important points:

■ answer your questions yourself if you can by researching and finding out for yourself

■ be careful – you must ask questions to gain understanding and not necessarily to get the answers; ask your classmates and anyone who will talk to you about your studies

■ if you are asking your teacher lots of questions which are actually variations of 'tell me the answer' or 'show me how to do this so that I can copy it' then you are learning passively – you should avoid this approach

■ take information which you have learned passively and use it actively by testing your knowledge in new and different situations by working through a range of examples

■ make links between the new ideas you are learning and the knowledge you already have to make sure you have connected the two

BRINGING IT ALL TOGETHER

If you remember, at the beginning of this chapter we defined the two layers of memory in the brain as follows:

■ there is **short-term memory** which stores information in your brain for only a limited period of time

■ there is **long-term memory** which retains information for a much longer period of time

The aim of learning is to fix knowledge and ways of working into the long-term memory and keep them there ready for new knowledge to be added to it and new methods to be developed.

The diagram on the next page summarises what you have been learning in this chapter. Do you find it effective as a resource to use in visual learning?

how the brain and memory work

Visual

'what you see'

Auditory

'what you hear'

Kinesthetic

'what you do'

Trash
Things that are forgotten: unused, unexplored ideas, information, and routine events.

VAK learning provides the information that is transmitted into the brain.

short-term memory

active learning
Active exploration and questioning of new information received into the short-term memory will help to move information and concepts from the short-term memory into the long-term memory. Here they are more likely to be retained and understood.

repeated passive learning
Repeated passive learning, where an activity or piece of knowledge is repeated again and again over a period of time, will move basic knowledge and skills from short-term memory into the long-term memory. The knowledge will not always be understood but repetition will make it stay in the long-term memory.

unusual event
A very unusual event will go straight into long-term memory. This is because exciting, frightening or extraordinary events are thought about and replayed in the mind again and again until you grasp what has happened – you actively engage in the memory of the event.

long-term memory

- existing concepts
- existing knowledge
- unusual events

TAKING CONTROL OF YOUR LEARNING

In this chapter you have learned that there are different ways for information to get into your short-term memory – and then most of the time you have to work to move the information into your long-term memory. You will move information to your long-term memory either by repetition or by questioning and analysing ideas and knowledge, linking them to ideas and knowledge that you already have in your long-term memory.

If you understand something very easily – such as a formula – do not assume that you will always remember it and be able to use it. Like all skills, you should practise using it so that it stays fresh in your mind for the exam.

the teacher/student roles in the learning process

So how can you take control of your learning? Isn't the teacher in charge? Well… yes and no. When you are in class then the teacher will set the work to be done and will choose the activities that take place. What you have to do is be active and engage in the learning by using the material that the teacher gives you and making it work in the best way for your learning preferences.

When you are studying outside of class time, you have more control of what you do and can take advantage of your learning preferences and strengths.

a need for the Visual, Auditory and Kinesthetic mix

Earlier in the chapter (page 33) we discussed the student who had filled in the Learning Journal in Chapter 2. We concluded that the student had not learned much from the lecture on control accounts. In fact the student had forgotten what was said and had to ask lots of questions in the next study period. When writing about the second study period, the student said:

> '*I couldn't remember anything from the lecture on 29 Sept! I had to keep looking at the slides. I wish I had made notes on the slides as I had to ask a lot of questions today.*'

The student had either not yet developed the ability to use the kinesthetic approach which would have suited him far better or he was not willing to experiment with new ways of working. Either way he was not able to make the best use of the material and activities from the session.

how to mix Visual, Auditory and Kinesthetic styles

If you can change the learning style that you use in lessons or when you are studying at home you will be more likely to stay engaged and work successfully. The following page sets out some tips for doing this:

- taking notes during a lecture will add kinesthetic to the visual and auditory learning of a lecture

- making notes when listening to podcasts or other auditory learning activities will constitute auditory and kinesthetic learning

- talking or reading aloud will add an auditory aspect to a study period, so long as it does not disturb other learners

All of these developments in your learning technique will mean that your learning is more active; this is because you are engaging with the material and working with it in different ways.

There is more information about note-taking in Chapter 6.

using passive learning

Passive learning may not always transfer ideas efficiently to the long-term memory, but it can be useful:

- memorising facts and information relating to accountancy, eg double-entry rules

- repeating the same calculation again and again, eg VAT calculations, invoice checking

Both of these examples make taking the assessment easier as you will be able to do routine tasks without having to think for too long about how to do them.

using active learning

Some activities are naturally active:

- in order to explain something well you have to think about the idea you are trying to get across – helping a fellow student by explaining an idea they are not sure of means you are taking part in active learning

- you have learned that some activities make you think about what you are doing and so these are also active

If you are taking part in an activity that is passive – perhaps your teacher is explaining something – **you can make the study period active** by:

- choosing key words and writing them down

- asking questions or writing down questions to ask later

- thinking about what the teacher is saying and trying to link it to knowledge and concepts that you already know, eg 'does he/she mean ....?'

- working through an example question with another student who needs help with it

what to do if you get stuck when learning

Sometimes when you study a topic you just cannot understand what you are trying to learn, for example what are debits or credits in double-entry.

If you find yourself up against a 'brick wall' like this and need thinking time, try the following active learning techniques:

- study the topic in short bursts or keep going away and coming back to the topic

- try to explain it to someone else – it does not matter if they do not get it either, the aim is to make you think about the topic

- go for a walk while you think about it

- take a break

When you come back to the topic after a break, ask your questions again, ask for help from your Study Buddies, online forums and your teachers.

Keep going backwards and forwards until you understand it. All this thinking will put the learning into the long-term memory, so do not give up.

Chapter Summary	

- 'VAK' stands for the Visual, Auditory and Kinesthetic styles of learning.

- 'Visual' = learning by seeing; 'Auditory' = learning by hearing; 'Kinesthetic' = learning by doing.

- You are likely to make use of at least two VAK learning styles during a study period.

- You will use your Learning Journal to identify which learning styles suit you best.

- You can adapt your methods of learning in periods of study to use your 'best' learning styles in order to improve your ability to learn.

- Learning can be active or passive.

- Passive learning is where you copy down information mechanically, listen to a lecture or practise the same calculation over and over again.

- Active learning is where you actively ask questions and try to work out what you are learning, linking to ideas and knowledge that you already have a good understanding of. Active learning is about engaging in learning.

■ Active learning can give deeper understanding and allow learning to be applied to different situations.

■ Having a deeper understanding of your present learning will help your future learning at higher levels or in different subjects.

■ Memory has both short-term and long-term storage; effective studying transfers knowledge and skills to the long-term section of your memory.

■ Actively engaging in learning will allow concepts and information to be transferred to long-term memory where information is held for a much longer time.

■ Passive learning will normally only put information into long-term memory in the case of frequently repeated pieces of learning.

■ Unusual events go into long-term memory because you actively engage in the memory of the event, replaying it in your mind again and again.

■ You can take control of your learning by engaging in an activity which can make a passive learning situation active, eg questioning a teacher in a lecture period or taking notes.

■ When you realise that you cannot understand a specific area of learning, use repeated short study sessions and other methods to keep revisiting the topic. If you get really stuck, ask your teacher for help and write down the response.

Key Terms		
	learning style (VAK)	three different processes used to take in information:
		Visual – you learn from what you see
		Auditory – you learn from what you hear
		Kinesthetic – you learn by doing something
	short-term memory	the part of your brain which receives information and stores it temporarily before passing it into long-term memory or discarding it
	long-term memory	the part of your brain which is able to retain and remember information for a long time which is most useful for effective learning
	passive learning	a learning process where you learn without thinking about the learning
	active learning	a learning process where you learn by actively questioning and thinking about the topic, engaging the brain to problem solve or link to earlier learning

Activities

Tick the correct answers for each question.

Note that there may be more than one correct answer to a question.

3.1 VAK stands for:

✔

(a)	Value Added Kinesthetic	
(b)	Visual Auditory Kinesthetic	
(c)	Value Auditory Kinesthetic	

3.2 An example of Kinesthetic learning is (tick one option):

✔

(a)	The teacher explaining something	
(b)	Listening to a Podcast	
(c)	Watching a video	
(d)	Interactive e-learning	

3.3 You can change learning situations to add different aspects of VAK.

Is this statement true or false?

✔

(a)	True	
(b)	False	

3.4   Ash has made an entry in his Learning Journal:

'I didn't understand what cross casting meant when the teacher explained it in class but when I read my text book and looked at the diagram, I got it straightaway.'

(i)   What learning style did he find difficult?   ✔

(a)	V	
(b)	A	
(c)	K	

(ii)   What learning style did he find helpful?   ✔

(a)	V	
(b)	A	
(c)	K	

3.5   Tom is trying to understand control accounts. He has entered the following into his journal:

'I couldn't understand why the Sales Day Book invoice totals go on the debit side of the Sales Ledger Control Account, I thought that Sales was a credit. Then my teacher made me draw some T accounts and enter some invoices directly into the accounts without the day book, then I understood.'

What learning style did Tom's teacher encourage him to use?   ✔

(a)	V	
(b)	A	
(c)	K	

3.6   Shannon is going to catch a train for an interview this afternoon and is checking the time of the train.

Into which part of Shannon's memory will the time of the train go?   ✔

(a)	Short-term memory	
(b)	Long-term memory	

3.7   Passive learning can be used to learn (tick the correct options):   ✔

(a)	Facts	
(b)	Theories	
(c)	Simple routine calculations	
(d)	Complicated calculations	

3.8   Examples of active learning are (tick the correct options):   ✔

(a)	Questioning	
(b)	Choosing key words to note	
(c)	Copying from the board	
(d)	Linking to concepts that are already understood	

3.9   Active learners have deeper understanding and will be better at studying higher levels of the qualification. Is this statement true or false?   ✔

(a)	True	
(a)	False	

3.10   Corrine has caught the same bus to College for the last year. In which part of Corinne's memory will be the time that the bus leaves?   ✔

(a)	Short-term memory	
(b)	Long-term memory	

3.11   Alex has decided to adopt active learning. He does not really understand the calculation for stock valuation in the costing unit. What will help Alex to understand? Tick the correct options.

✔

(a)	Keep trying the calculation in different ways until he gets the correct answer	
(b)	Talk about it with Rose, his Study Buddy	
(c)	Try to explain the calculation to a non-accounting friend	
(d)	Have a go, get an answer and compare it with Rose's answer	
(e)	Ask Rose to show him her answer	

3.12   You can personally control your learning. Is this statement true or false?

✔

(a)	True	
(b)	False	

4 Learning activities

this chapter covers...

This chapter describes in detail the range of different methods of learning that you can use in your studies so that you will be able to decide which will suit you best. The areas the chapter covers are:

- *what is meant by 'engaging in learning'*

- *the advantages and disadvantages of learning in groups*

- *different ways of learning as part of a group*

- *the benefits of role play*

- *how working in pairs is both different and the same as working in a group or as an individual*

- *the benefits of having study buddies*

- *how to work effectively on your own*

- *different types of questions and examples and their benefits*

- *the range of ways in which you can learn electronically*

- *the benefits of learning electronically and the challenges you can meet when learning this way*

TYPES OF LEARNING ACTIVITY

getting 'engaged' in your learning

In the last chapter you learned about the VAK (Visual, Auditory, Kinesthetic) styles of learning and how to understand and remember information.

We will now describe the different ways of learning that you can 'engage' in.

to 'engage in' learning means becoming involved and interested in it

Different activities use different combinations of the VAK styles. By trying out a range of different types of activity, you can change the mix of VAK styles you are good at using and this may help you to understand and remember new learning better.

The greater the variety of learning activities and methods you use, the more engaged you can be and this will make you more likely to learn. If you keep using the same method of learning it can be hard to keep your attention on what you are trying to do.

If you make a list of different types of learning activity you might come up with something like this:

■ learning in groups

■ learning in pairs

■ learning on your own with paper-based material

■ learning on your own electronically with a computer

In the rest of this chapter we will explain in detail:

■ the different types of activity

■ how to identify which types of activity are best for you

LEARNING IN GROUPS

Most of your learning has probably been in classrooms where you will have taken part in group work as well as working on tasks individually.

Group work allows you to discuss and share information. It also allows you to share ideas and solve problems together with your classmates. Group work involves a mix of visual, auditory and kinesthetic styles.

advantages of learning in groups

Being able to work in groups and teams is important in the classroom and the workplace because it has the following advantages:

- you can discuss problems to find solutions
- you can question what other group members think – you should always do this in a polite and positive way
- you can have your thoughts and opinions questioned by other members of the group – explaining what you think can help you to understand it better
- you can share out tasks
- your strengths can be used by the group
- the group can support you in areas you need to develop
- you can put forward your own ideas
- you can learn to accept criticism from others

disadvantages of working in groups

There are also drawbacks to working in groups. These include:

- some members of the group may not be as interested and engaged in the work as others so they might not work so hard; others might not take a full part in the group work because they are shy, afraid of getting things wrong or prefer to work on their own
- everyone will need to be engaged and working to meet their deadlines if the group is to finish their work on time
- if you only stick to your strong areas during group work and do not get involved in doing new activities – in which you are not so strong – you might miss valuable chances to improve your skills

We will now examine some of the activities you may do in groups.

group discussions

 A group discussion is where you and a few other students are asked to discuss a question or problem. Usually you will all discuss the same question or topic in small groups and then tell the whole class what your conclusions are.

Think about the advantages and disadvantages of group work stated above. How do you think that they apply to a group discussion?

the advantages of a group discussion

- discussing a problem will help you to see the problem in different ways as everyone has different viewpoints

- tasks such as note taking and feeding back to the whole class may be shared

- one member of the group will normally take a leader or 'chairperson' role

- every member of the group will bring their own strengths to each task so the group will become stronger by combining these strengths

potential challenges with group discussions

- sometimes some students will not get involved in group discussions but will let the conversation go on without taking part much – this is often because they are shy and are not confident enough to speak; it may also be because they do not wish to engage with the topic that is being discussed because they do not like it or do not know about it

- the quality and the number of topics covered in your discussion might be affected if some members of the group do not engage and take part

- some students can hide the fact that they do not like or feel confident in doing certain tasks when they are in a group – it may always be the same students taking the notes, leading the discussion or giving feedback to the class; as a result the students who do not take part will not be able to improve these skills if they avoid practising them

- some members of the group may often criticise other members – this happens in all types of group (including families!); other members must learn to accept criticism – the criticism may in fact be constructive and helpful if it makes people see things from a different point of view!

engaging in a group discussion to improve your learning

Active learners will always have something to say in a group discussion. If you want to actively engage in this type of learning you should do one of the following:

- take part in the discussion by exchanging your ideas and knowledge and do not let one or two people take over the discussion

- if you do not know anything about the subject being discussed, you should ask questions to help you to understand – by asking questions you help yourself to learn and you help those answering the questions to learn because they have to think about how to answer

- take the role of note taker – this will help you to actively engage in the group; summarising the main points in your own words will help you to learn what you have written

- take the role of feeding back from your individual group to the class group – this will ensure that you understand the discussion enough to tell others about what was discussed and agreed

role play

Sometimes a group discussion includes an element of role play.

role play is where members of a group take on different roles to act out a situation

Some students may say that they dislike role play: they feel uncomfortable in an acting role; but fully engaging in a situation by 'getting into the part' will certainly improve their learning.

Example:

Role play involving an ethical problem – fiddling the expenses

A line manager asks an accounts assistant to enter a large expense claim in the accounts. The assistant knows that it is a bill for a non-business weekend away for the manager and his partner.

In other words, the accounts assistant knows that the claim is not a business expense and the manager will be fiddling the books and defrauding the business.

What does the accounts assistant do . . .

Do as she is told and do nothing?

Tell the line manager that she cannot fiddle the books?

Tell the line manager that he should not fiddle the books?

Do as she is told and afterwards tell a senior manager?

Whether you are acting out one of the roles or are watching others acting out the roles, you are more likely to understand the pressure that the manager can put onto the clerk because the manager has authority over the accounts assistant.

If you are watching any type of role play, you need to think about how you would feel and what you would say if you were playing one of the roles.

Note that role play:

■ uses more in the way of visual and kinesthetic learning styles when compared with simple group discussion because the whole group becomes more involved in the situation which seems so 'real'

■ will encourage the whole group to become more actively engaged in the discussion which follows the role play and so the students are more likely to remember the discussion and understand the underlying concepts

group projects

At times during your studies, you will be asked to work with others on a project over a long period of time. It may be that you will work as a group to find information and to present it to the class at a later date, possibly after a few days, possibly after a few weeks.

When undertaking a project, as a member of a group you will have to decide on roles, take on tasks and discuss the planned outcomes.

The strengths and challenges of group working will encourage and strengthen your personal development.

WORKING IN PAIRS

 Working in pairs is a really good way of learning. It is more personal and is more focused on you and your partner. But as in any partnership each partner must be able to get on with the 'other half' and contribute fully. If one person in a pair does most of the work, it usually does not last for long!

Almost all learning activities can be done by a pair:

- a pair is in effect a small group, so many group activities can be done in pairs

- individual type activities can be done working together in pairs

- you may decide to work on a given task independently and then compare answers for confidence

- you may share a workspace but decide that you want to do individual work when you are told to work with someone else as a pair; although this will mean that you will keep each other company, you are likely to learn much more if you actively work together and share the task

Study Buddies

a Study Buddy is a partner – another student – with whom you study

Study Buddies work together – either in pairs or in small groups – to learn effectively by helping each other in a variety of ways:

- meeting up to study outside class at agreed times

- supporting each other by explaining or discussing problems

- taking different areas to research and sharing the results to save time

- testing each other's knowledge

The last bullet point on the previous page – testing knowledge with someone else – is particularly useful because it is very **active** learning. If you think about this type of interaction between two people, it involves all three learning styles:

- **visual** – seeing the learning material on paper or on screen

- **auditory** – hearing the 'buddy' ask the question and confirm the answer

- **kinesthetic** – working together and organising tasks, research and notes and planning responses to questions

Testing is a good way of learning and remembering the knowledge parts of the qualification, eg which accounts are expenses and which are liabilities.

INDIVIDUAL STUDY

Taking advantage of all learning situations is the key to effective learning. Individual study can involve a wide range of activities:

- reading books and journals

- practising questions

- interactive online learning – e-learning

We will now describe these various activities, the various ways in which they use the VAK learning styles, and how students can actively engage in them.

reading books and journals

 Reading is a very important way of learning and has been used for thousands of years. The basic reading process – just scanning the page and using your brain to make sense of the words – is **visual** only and **passive**. This process will place the information in your short-term memory only. But actively engaging with the book, journal, or whatever you are reading, can make reading kinesthetic and more effective. You should:

- identify what seems useful and important, making notes on paper or on a computer or tablet

- write key words or summaries of useful sections of the text

- pause periodically to think about what you have read, linking it to what you already know about the topic

- if you own the book or journal, make notes in the margins, and highlight important areas of the text

■ take regular breaks when you are reading to allow you to absorb what you have read

■ read again what you have written on a regular basis

You will see that these activities have made your reading more **active** and less **passive**. The way in which you have to write notes and think about what you have read and then verbalise your thoughts makes the learning very **active** and will help to place the information in your long-term memory. If you have a Study Buddy you can literally 'compare notes'. This makes the learning auditory and kinesthetic as well as visual.

The techniques, uses and advantages of note-taking are explained in more detail in Chapter 6 (pages 84-101).

practising questions

When studying accounting and business you will have to do many practice questions as part of your individual learning.

These are likely to include:

■ **Simple calculations** – where you are given numbers to practice specific calculations such as calculating the VAT at 20% on an invoice.

Carrying out a simple calculation is essentially a **passive** activity.

■ **Problem solving** – where you are given a problem and some information and asked to find a solution. This is different from the simple calculation because you are having to identify the information that you need and then decide how to use the information to get the solution. For example, you may know how to work out the VAT with a settlement discount on an invoice for £1,000, but you may be given an invoice where you have to calculate when and how much to pay from the details on the invoice, taking into account any settlement discount available.

■ **Scenario questions** – in a scenario you may take the role of a person working in a firm which is described in full for you. For example, you may be given details of price lists, discount agreements and purchase orders and have to work out how much to charge a customer, calculating the correct amount for an invoice, then issue a credit note for returned goods and subsequently send out a statement.

Problem solving and scenario questions are essentially **active**: you have to think about them and understand what is happening in each situation.

All of these types of individual study are **visual** and **kinesthetic**. To make these types **auditory** you could either discuss the problems with a Study Buddy, or alternatively, read out and record the questions and then play the recording back to yourself.

it is good to make mistakes

Getting questions wrong and then correcting them is an excellent way of learning. You are more likely to retain the knowledge than if you just wait until someone shows you how to do the question. This is because the attempt and correction are active and just being told how to answer the question is passive. Give each question a go, and do not worry if you get it wrong.

interactive online learning – e-learning

 Reading a book has been a tried and tested method of learning over thousands of years, but electronic learning – **e-learning**, – is a comparatively new development which has now become accepted as a popular and **active** form of learning.

You learn electronically in a number of different ways:

- researching information – eg using Google

- completing interactive learning modules – ie online 'lessons'

- taking online interactive tests and quizzes

- doing online puzzles – eg crosswords

- watching videos (eg from YouTube)

- listening to podcasts

- taking part in webinars and online student forums

- reading and writing blogs and watching or creating video blogs or 'vlogs'

One of the reasons that e-learning is so successful is the way it is usually split into manageable chunks of learning: most information on the internet or available electronically is designed for quick access and quick completion.

researching information

Because of the speed at which you can access information and the choices that you make when researching electronically, the learning in this case is kinesthetic. It may also be visual and auditory, depending on what your research results are.

Look below at one result of an online search for e-learning.

Osborne Books - Online Learning
www.osbornebooks.co.uk/elearning ▾
"Brilliant **books** and **elearning**, proved invaluable for my studies so far." "Excellent **books** and
... WR2 5HP, UK T: 01905 748071 E: **books@osbornebooks**.co.uk.

Warning! Anyone can put material on the internet; the content is not checked to see if it is correct or has been written by an expert. It is very important that you always check every information source very carefully and only select research materials from sources that can be trusted to be correct.

interactive learning modules

Online learning modules are short lessons which can provide information and also test your knowledge as you go along, when you want, where you want and at your own pace.

The learning styles are both **visual** and **kinesthetic**: you read the information and often have to answer questions. Sometimes the modules include video clips – eg a tutor explaining a topic – which will introduce an element of **auditory** learning (see page 60 for further discussion of video).

Interactive learning modules can be done in pairs or larger groups (eg when the teacher projects the learning module on a screen in the classroom) and will stimulate discussion and increase **auditory** and **kinesthetic** input.

The AAT website www.aat.org.uk//training/study-support has a number of online learning modules for the Units you are studying. The example below (for this Unit) is testing a student's knowledge of the sources of information.

online interactive tests and quizzes

Students are also able to carry out individual study by taking online tests and practice assessments and engaging in e-learning. Getting used to computer-based assessments is an important part of the learning process.

Testing your knowledge – either online or by other means – means that you will find out exactly how much you know. You can learn much by testing yourself and, when you get it wrong, actively thinking about the correct answer, trying to work out why you were wrong.

Here is a sample question from an online practice assessment produced by Osborne Books for the Bookkeeping 1 Unit you will be studying:

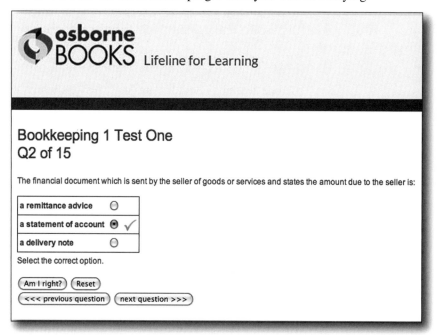

Tests for the AAT accounting Units are available free of charge from www.osbornebooks.co.uk/elearning

The main advantage of doing tests and quizzes electronically are:

■ you can access them at a convenient time for you

■ the computer marks the questions and gives you quick feedback

■ you can repeat tests and there is often more than one test for each area of learning

Tests and quizzes are **visual** and **kinesthetic** and you actively engage in them. You can get maximum benefit from tests and quizzes if you:

■ note down the questions and topic areas that you get wrong and the reasons why

■ study those topics again fully

■ test yourself again

Remember that these questions may only test a small percentage of each of the topic areas.

If you do find that you still need to develop your skills further in certain areas it is very important that you return to that topic and revise it all in depth so that you will be ready for any question that you may have to answer.

online puzzles

Some people do not think that doing puzzles or games are important ways of learning, but they are actually two of the best ways of doing active learning because they are both **visual** and **kinesthetic**. Sudoku and cryptic crosswords can be very challenging puzzles and are very popular with adults – so remember that puzzles are not just 'games for kids'.

Crosswords can be set up online as a form of e-learning themed to a specific area of study; they are very helpful because they are:

■ **visual** – very often a pattern of words set up in a particular shape can be remembered more easily as your memory will recall **where** the words are and also **what** the words are

■ **kinesthetic** – the process of thinking about the possible words and the then filling them in on the screen is active; other activities include pressing a 'hint' button to provide some help – and, of course, like any crosswords it can be completed by a group of people discussing the clues and providing possible solutions between them

The example below shows an online interactive crossword available at (www.osbornebooks.co.uk) for AAT Unit Bookkeeping 1.

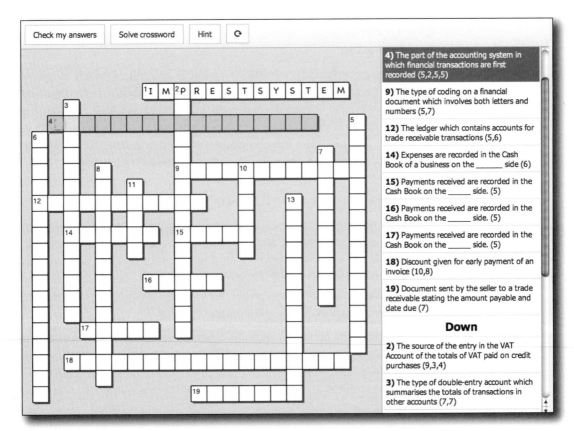

video, YouTube and podcasts

Students are increasingly using **video** to help them learn. The main sources are firstly the learning providers who provide online access through their portals to lectures on video, and secondly the 'worldwide web' itself. One video site that is especially popular is YouTube (www.youtube.com) – not only for its entertainment value but also as an aid to learning.

Try doing a search on YouTube for 'double-entry bookkeeping' or 'study skills' and you will see how much material is available. Good ways to tell whether a YouTube video is of high quality and provides useful information are to see how many 'hits' or 'viewings' it has received, the comments of other viewers on the webpage – and also to note when it was posted.

Any video, unless it is silent, engages you **passively** in both **visual** and **auditory** styles of learning. You can also make it **kinesthetic** by actively taking notes of the content and discussing it with others. The main advantages of video are:

■ they tend to be short and manageable 'chunks' of learning

■ you can pause the video if you need to, either to go back if you are losing the thread, to ask questions about the content or to write down the main points

■ it is sometimes easier to remember information that has been spoken

■ you are free to discuss the content at any time if a group of you watch the video together

Podcasts were originally introduced as audio recordings which could be listened to on an iPod, ie 'on the go'. The content might be for entertainment (radio programmes) or learning materials such as lessons which are available in spoken form for use at home or when travelling. Podcasts are still in use for training purposes and are obviously **auditory** in nature. Nowadays the term 'podcast' has been expanded to include video as well as sound.

webinars and student forums

Webinars are online lectures or meetings hosted by one individual or organisation. The number of students may be 1 or 2 or it may be hundreds. You learn in the same way as you would at school or college, but you do it from your own home or when at work. Some webinars allow questions to be entered online and some allow verbal discussions between the presenter and the students, which makes the process more **active.**

Online forums are online 'chat rooms' where students can ask each other for help outside lesson sessions. A good online forum can be like having a hundred study buddies ready to help you when you are stuck. The more that you engage with the learning, the more you will learn and retain. An online forum is only as good as its members – but it can be very good.

Chapter Summary

- Engaging in learning means becoming involved and interested in it.

- Using a range of activities will make learning more interesting and help to keep your learning active.

- You can change learning situations to make them have a greater VAK range and to change from active to passive learning.

- Group work helps learning with active discussions and sharing information.

- Everyone in a group must engage to get the most out of the learning situation.

- You must make sure that you strengthen the areas and skills you need to develop by being active and engaging rather than letting other group members take the lead.

- Role play is useful as it brings scenarios to life – if everyone engages fully.

- Working in pairs is a focused way of learning.

- Study Buddies can be very valuable with study help and in motivating you to succeed.

- You can change reading from a passive learning activity to an active one by engaging with the content.

- Problem solving and scenario questions are active and likely to help you learn in the long term – even if they can be challenging activities!

- E-learning is useful, active and convenient.

- A range of e-learning modules, tests and quizzes have been written especially for your AAT units.

- When you get questions wrong in a particular topic, you must go away and study the topic again – do not just learn the answers on the e-learning tests, the questions in the exam may be different to the ones you are attempting.

- Online forums can be like having a hundred Study Buddies.

Key Terms	**engaging in learning**	becoming involved and interested in your learning
	passive learning	a learning process where you learn without thinking about the learning
	active learning	a learning process where you learn by actively questioning and thinking about the topic, engaging the brain to problem solve or link to earlier learning
	role play	a situation where a scenario is acted out by two or more people, often watched by others, to help everyone understand a problem such as the pressure a manager can put on a member of staff
	study buddy	a partner student with whom you study, both of you helping each other to learn
	simple calculation	where you are specifically told 'use these numbers to calculate in this way' – this is passive learning
	problem solving	where you have some information and have to identify what information to use to solve a problem – this is active learning
	scenario questions	where you take on the role of a person working in an imaginary business and have to complete tasks required by the job – this is active learning
	e-learning	learning online, either carrying out research or by engaging with interactive learning materials
	e-learning modules	online learning modules written for specific subjects or learning situations, including information and quizzes and tests
	webinars	online lectures or meetings logged into by anything from two people to hundreds of people
	online forums	online chat rooms where students can ask each other for help

Activities

4.1 Write in the appropriate columns in the table below whether the activities are:

(a) Visual, Auditory and/or Kinesthetic (write 'V', 'A' or 'K' or a combination of these letters)

(b) Active or Passive (write 'P' or 'A')

The first one has already been completed for you:

Learning Activity	VAK?	Active or Passive?
Watching a video presentation or film	VA	P
Practising the same calculation (with different numbers) over and over again		
Practice questions that need thinking about		
Reading		
Teacher talking or lecturing		
Working on a problem in pairs		
Research on a computer		
Look at a given computer website		
Demonstration – you are shown how to do something		
You explain or demonstrate to another person		
Research using books and journals		
Group discussion		
Pair discussion		
Scenario or case studies done individually		
Scenario or case studies done in pairs		
Scenario or case studies done in groups		
Multiple choice quiz		
Puzzles		
Checking other students' work		
You give a presentation to the class on your own		
You are part of a group presenting information to the class		
Preparing researched information to present to the class		

There may be more than one correct answer for the questions below which involve option choices.

4.2   If Chelsea does not engage in group work, what are the consequences?   ✔

(a)	None	
(b)	The group work may be delayed or not as good as it could have been	
(c)	Chelsea learns less than she would have learned if she had engaged	

4.3   Mary has taken on the role of note taker in a group discussion. Mary is: ✔

(a)	Learning actively	
(b)	Learning passively	

4.4   If you feed back to the class as a whole, you have to actively think about: ✔

(a)	What to say	
(b)	How to explain what you are going to say	
(c)	Your personal appearance	

4.5   Reading or looking at a webpage can be visual and passive. How can you make it kinesthetic and active? Describe two ways in which you might be able to do this.

4.6   Hugh and his friends are having a discussion about a workplace situation. They decide that they will act out the situation to help them to understand it. Explain how this will improve their learning

(a)   in terms of VAK

(b)   in terms of active and passive learning

4.7   Sarah wants to know about the advantages of having a Study Buddy.
What should you tell her?   ✔

(a)	You feel supported	
(b)	You have someone to study with	
(c)	None – you think that you prefer to work on your own	
(d)	You can do each other's homework for areas that each finds difficult	

4.8 Problem solving and scenario questions can be more challenging than other types of question. ✔

(a)	True	
(b)	False	

4.9 Your learning is likely to be deeper and more thorough when you do problem solving or scenario questions. ✔

(a)	True	
(b)	False	

4.10 Patrick is planning to do the AAT e-learning modules for the Study Skills Unit. Patrick can do these modules: ✔

(a)	At home	
(b)	At college	
(c)	Only at a specific time	
(d)	At any time that is convenient to Patrick	

4.11 Special is doing the AAT's Green Light tests. She finds them helpful because: ✔

(a)	They make her think	
(b)	She has to get them fully correct to get the mark	
(c)	They highlight areas that she needs to study	
(d)	They do not help because she finds them too hard	

4.12 Usman is taking part in an online forum. Why do you think that he finds it helpful?

Give two reasons why the forum might be able to help develop his learning.

4.13 Kit-Chi is listening to a podcast while going home on the train. She knows that it is passive learning but she finds it difficult to write while travelling. What can she do to make her learning active?

Give two suggestions for making her learning active on her daily commute.

5 Information gathering

this chapter covers...

This chapter describes in detail how you collect and organise the information you deal with in your studies. The main areas the chapter covers are:

- ■ *the main stages of finding information which you will be able to use*

- ■ *the range of sources that you will find helpful for your studies in accounting and business*

- ■ *ways in which you can check information – including the sources of information and surveys that have been carried out*

- ■ *making sure that the information is relevant*

- ■ *how to organise your information*

- ■ *how to use references to explain where your information came from*

- ■ *the concepts of copyright and intellectual property*

- ■ *the need to avoid plagiarism – ie using other people's material without giving a reference which explains that it is not your own*

DEALING WITH INFORMATION

the main stages

When you need to find out information as part of your learning – eg when you are writing a project – you will need to think about how you are going to:

■ find the **source** of the information you need – ie where it comes from

■ obtain the **correct information** in a form you can use – eg make notes or copy and paste text

■ **store** the information so that you can find and **use it** easily, eg on your computer or in a notepad

This may all sound easy and obvious, but you need to be organised in the way you find the information and store it in a place where you can easily find it. You will need to follow all these steps if you are to complete your research and ensure that your work is accurate and finished on time. Study the flow diagram below.

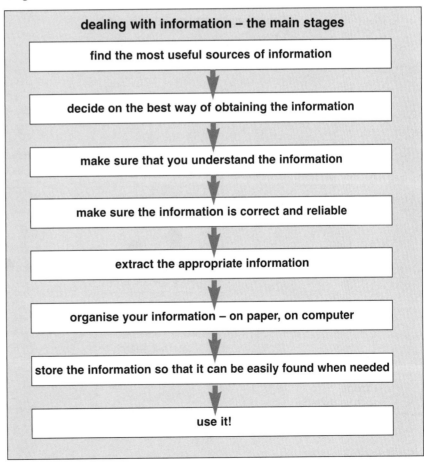

dealing with information – the main stages

find the most useful sources of information

decide on the best way of obtaining the information

make sure that you understand the information

make sure the information is correct and reliable

extract the appropriate information

organise your information – on paper, on computer

store the information so that it can be easily found when needed

use it!

locating your sources

The course that you are studying is focused on the accounting and business environment. Where will you find information relating to this? If you carry out a 'brainstorming' exercise you may come up with the following list:

- books, manuals, magazine articles, reports containing text, pictures and diagrams

- the internet, using search engines such as Google

- archive records (stored records no longer in current use)

- family and contacts

- organised work experience, part-time jobs

- teachers and visiting speakers from the business world

In this list you will see that there are three main types of information source:

- **paper-based information**

- **digital information**, eg information from the internet

- **personal contact** and experience

This is shown in the diagram below.

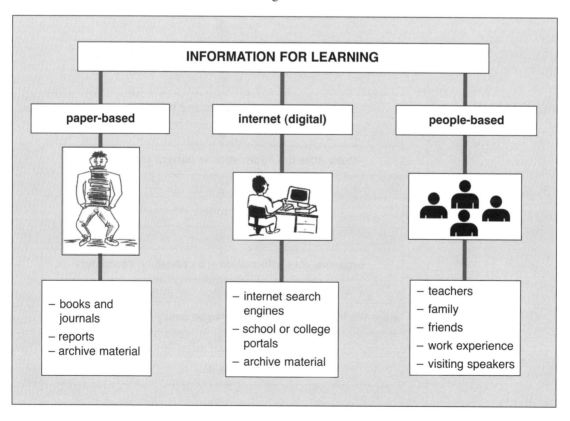

The diagram on the previous page could be used for any subject that you are studying, but it is important to know about the specific sources for **accounting and business**.

paper-based sources for accounting and business

■ **textbooks** – for example, this book and other books in the Osborne Books Level 2 Accounting and Business Series

■ **magazines** – for example the AAT 'Accounting Technician' has relevant articles to help with your studies

■ **newspapers** – these have regular finance and business sections

Libraries are a good place to visit for paper-based sources. They will also normally have computers available to research online sources and staff to help you with your searches or recommend useful books or journals.

Libraries are also likely to have archived material, for example past issues of journals and reports. This used to be kept in paper format but is now more likely to be available as digitised content viewable on screen.

digital sources for accounting and business

You should always use a trusted Search Engine such as Google or Bing when you are doing online research. You will also get more accurate results if you are careful about the words you type in when you do your search and this means using the right 'key words'. Try the following:

'business education' – www.bized.co.uk is recommended

Once you get your search results it is always worth asking teaching or library staff if the source you have found is trusted and reliable. Another source is a college's or school's **intranet** (ie internal internet) which may be able to provide the required learning material.

When researching accounting online be sure that you are looking at information for **UK** accounting. You can do this by checking what currency is in use or looking for '.co.uk' at the end of the web address.

YouTube can also be a source of useful 'how to' videos (see page 60).

HOW GOOD IS THE INFORMATION?

It is very important that the information sources you use in your research and writing are reliable. The source is where the information has originally come from. Just because someone has said or written something does not make it fact. Certain information that has been published, both on paper and on the internet, has been shown to be inaccurate and misleading.

how do you tell if written information is correct?

The first thing to look at is the source of the information. Who said it or wrote it? To make sure that your information has come from a valid and reliable source, in other words a source that you can trust, you should check the following:

- do you know the name of the author or the publisher?

- if you are looking online, is the website an official website like HMRC (HM Revenue & Customs) or GOV.UK (the official site for Government services and information) or is it one you know nothing about?

- if you cannot find who is responsible for the information then you may not be able to trust the information

- is the source an advertisement or marketing material which is trying to sell you something?

- check the accuracy of the information by consulting two independent sources as a 'double check' - this is known as **triangulation**

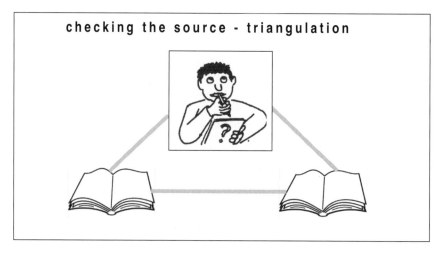

checking the source - triangulation

taking care over survey results

Surveys often produce statistics as their results – for example 'eight out of ten cat owners liked Kittibits', or '75% of people surveyed agreed'. Often you might need to be careful about using these types of surveys – there is a saying:

'There are three kinds of lies: lies, damned lies and statistics'

Statistics often come from surveys. Like articles, if a survey is paid for by a person or company that is likely to benefit from one result and be damaged by another result, do you think that you can trust the results of the survey?

Study the example on the next page.

Example:

Softsip Ltd – skewing the survey results

Softsip Ltd is a manufacturer of soft drinks.

It wishes to promote an advertising campaign about a recently launched fruit-based drink, Fruitydelight.

A member of Softsip's sales team is told to set up a stand in a busy supermarket and ask passing shoppers if they would like to sample the soft drink free of charge. The sales rep asks everyone who tries the drink whether they like it. 14% say that they like it.

The next day another sales rep stands in the same place in the supermarket and again offers a free sample to the shoppers. This time each of the customers who tries the drink is given a free £5 voucher for any Softsip product. They are then asked for their opinion of the drink in a short survey.

This time 31% of the people say that they like the drink.

An advert eventually appears in the press claiming that Fruitydelight was 'liked by over 30% of people who tried it for the first time.'

Do you think this is fair practice on the part of Softsip Limited? Do you think this information is reliable?

If information is not reliable because of unfair practice, as in the example above, we say that it is 'biased'. Not all surveys are biased. There are companies who specialise in market surveys, eg Ipsos MORI, Mintel, Gallup; their reputation relies on accuracy. The UK Government Office for National Statistics is also a reliable source of statistical information.

The table below gives examples of sources of information to trust and sources which may be less reliable and need to be checked for validity – because the source may be biased.

sources to trust	sources to check up on
a book recommended by your teacher	an old edition of a textbook going cheap from another student
a book by a well-known author from a respected publisher	books sold by an online retailer which sells both new and old books
VAT information provided by the Government HMRC website	VAT advice offered by a friend of a friend
an Open University lecture on business finance seen on the TV	a meeting with a local firm selling hire purchase finance

IS THE INFORMATION RELEVANT?

One of the main problems about information in this digital age is that there is often too much of it. Not only do you have to check that it is accurate and can be trusted, you also need to check that the information is at the correct level of detail and depth for your research.

To help you in this process you must ask yourself the following questions:

- is the information **relevant** to what I am looking for?

- do I **understand** what it says?

- does it come from a **trusted** source?

This process is illustrated in the Example which follows.

Example:

Researching information about Value Added Tax

You have been asked to research information about how the rates of UK Value Added Tax sometimes vary from year to year. Where will you go to look for the information? Assume that you are going to use your textbook and the internet. Before you ask or look for the information you will need to:

- Identify the precise question(s) that you need to answer, for example:

  'What is the current rate of standard VAT in the UK and when has it changed over the last few years?'

- Identify the possible sources, thinking about how reliable they may be:

  - paper-based sources: textbooks, information leaflets

  - websites: do a search and try a variety of sites, eg www.hmrc.gov.uk

When you have chosen your sources and asked your questions, you will need to look at the information that you have found and see if it is reliable. For example, one article states that:

  - VAT changed to 15% on 1 Dec 2008

  - VAT returned to 17.5 % on 1 January 2010

  - VAT increased to 20% on 4 January 2011

  - VAT changed from 21% to 23% on 1 January 2012

The last bullet point seems to be wrong – you do not recall seeing a 21% or 23% rate quoted before. It is wrong. You know because you check this information against other sources, eg your textbook and www.hmrc.gov.uk.

The information is incorrect as far as the UK is concerned: a Google search on '23% VAT' shows that the 23% rate of VAT is charged in Ireland.

The example on the previous page shows that you must be careful to choose the right information and use it carefully. You should make sure that you can justify your use of information by showing that the sources are reliable; this is done by **referencing**, ie by quoting the sources that you use (see page 74).

ORGANISING YOUR INFORMATION

When you have collected the information for your learning, you should have made sure that it is . . .

■ reliable

■ valid

■ understandable

■ relevant

You will also then need to sort it and store it in an organised way so that it is readily and easily accessible whenever you need it.

Some people are well organised with a tidy desk, some are disorganised and untidy. The message here is that you must have an organised system for storing your information so that you can access it easily and quickly when you need it. Different types of information need different types of storage:

■ Storage of **paper-based material** can be organised by using:

– well-labelled box files or A4 folders for individual projects or Units

– desk trays for 'stuff not done' and 'work in progress'

– 'work completed' should be safely stored where it can easily be found

– indexed 'archive' boxes or filing cabinets for no longer used material

■ Storage and archiving of **electronic material** is more risky as the storage device (eg USB stick, portable hard disk, or remote location backup) may fail and so multiple back-up in different storage media is highly recommended.

■ As you save **electronic documents** it is important that you keep them in an organised system – your computer desktop should always be tidy with:

– files given logical names which clearly say what they are

– groups of similar files, eg project work, stored in clearly named folders

– back-up systems to stop you overwriting your work, eg saving project files as you go along: 'Project 1 version 1', 'Project 1 version 2' etc

During your course you may be asked to provide screenshots proving that you are able to store your electronic documents in a well-organised way. Study the screenshot of the sales spreadsheets on the next page.

screenshot of organisation of folders for sales spreadsheets

▼ 📁 Sales spreadsheets ←──────────────┐   **main folder**
   ▶ 📁 2008–2010 ←──────────┐   │   containing all sales spreadsheet files
   ▶ 📁 2011 ←──────────────┐   │
   ▶ 📁 2012 ←──────────────┐   │
   ▶ 📁 2013 ←──────────────┐   │   **year folders** for sales spreadsheet files,
   ▼ 📁 2014 ←──────────────┘   │   organised in year order
      ▶ 📁 01 January 2014 ←──┐
      ▶ 📁 02 February 2014 ←─┤   **month folders** for sales spreadsheet files,
      ▶ 📁 03 March 2014 ←────┤   given consecutive numbers (eg January is
      ▶ 📁 04 April 2014 ←────┤   '01') so that they will show in month order
      ▶ 📁 05 May 2014 ←──────┤   rather than alphabetical order, making
      ▶ 📁 06 June 2014 ←─────┤   them much easier to locate
      ▶ 📁 07 July 2014 ←─────┤
      ▶ 📁 08 August 2014 ←───┤
      ▶ 📁 09 September 2014 ←─┘

the organisation of information in business

The principles of efficient organisation of information explained on the previous page will also apply to an accounts department of a business, for example:

- **filing** of **current paper documents**: invoices, receipts, orders, letters, bank statements

- secure and indexed **archiving** of paper documents which are no longer current – these are normally retained for at least six years

- secure back up of current and archived **electronic data** both on and off the business premises

REFERENCING YOUR INFORMATION SOURCES

the need to reference information

On the last page we saw that you need to be organised in collecting and storing paper-based and electronic information. It is also important to be able to track your sources of information for a number of reasons:

- you may need to refer back to the information to check what you have written

- your assessor may need to refer back to the information to check what you have written

- if the sources of your research are not made clear to your assessor, you will need to prove that you have not copied it or made it up

methods of referencing – books and journals

For the Level 2 Study Skills Unit it is suggested that you use the following method of referencing your source:

- the **title** of your source – eg book title, magazine title
- the name(s) of the **author(s)** of your source
- the **date** of publication of the source
- the **page number(s)** of the material

You should put the reference to the source immediately after any quotation or information you use from it. Set out below are example references to provide you with all the details you will need.

Example: referencing book sources

Alexi, a Level 2 accountancy student has identified a quote to use in her assignment. The quote is a key term from her 'Working in Accounting and Finance Tutorial' textbook and she has put it in her text like this:

'achieving the right result with the minimum of wasted time, effort or expense.'

The reference reads as follows:

(Working in Accounting and Finance Tutorial, M. Fardon, 2013, p30.)

Alexi has referenced the quotation by putting the book title, author, year of publication and page number in brackets after the quote.

If an article from a journal is being quoted, it is a good idea also to include the name of the article at the beginning of the reference and follow it with the name of the journal and then the name of the author, as shown below:

Example: referencing article sources

Alexi has also quoted from an article 'Developments in contactless payments' written by W. Gatz in the magazine 'Financial Technology World':

'Contactless cards provide a faster, more convenient way to pay for purchases of up to £20.'

The reference following the quotation will be as follows:

('Developments in contactless payments', Financial Technology World, W. Gatz, 16 May 2014, p14.)

methods of referencing – electronic sources

You may also need to refer to information taken from the internet. The same principles that you used when quoting paper-based sources apply. The details you will need are:

- the **website link** copied from the computer screen
- the **date** that you accessed the information

Hint: if you are writing an assessment which is in electronic format, eg a Word file, which will also be seen onscreen by your assessor, you should copy and paste the link to the online material so that you can (or the assessor) go straight to the source of information.

An example of an online source is shown below:

Example: referencing online sources

Alexi is having difficulty with her double-entry and has been looking for online back-up reading. Her teacher has recommended an online exercise provided by Biz/ed called 'Pepe's Pizza Parlour'. Alexi does an online search and finds the appropriate link. She quotes the following from this exercise:

'The total value of the accounts in credit must equal the total value of the accounts in debit.'

She then writes the following reference:

(http://www.bized.co.uk/learn/business/accounting/busaccounts/pizza/stufiftn.htm. Accessed 20 May 2014)

a note on the Harvard referencing system

When doing your reading you may come across a more complex referencing system that is widely used in the educational world – the **Harvard** system. You do not need to use it for your AAT assessments at Level 2 but it is useful to know how it works when you are researching.

The Harvard system includes the following details in the following order:

- author's last name followed by initials
- year of publication
- title of book (in italics) and edition number
- place of publication (the town or city)
- the publisher

If Alexi used the Harvard referencing system all the references would be grouped together at the end of her work as an alphabetical list like this:

Fardon, M. (2013). *Working Effectively in Accounting and Finance.* Worcester: Osborne Books.

References within the text would read 'Fardon, 2013, p. 30'.

intellectual property, copyright and plagiarism

One of the reasons for referencing the material and quotations you use in your assessment is that you are stating that you have not written it yourself and you are using it to provide evidence and back-up for your work.

This is not a problem, it is exactly what you should do. Using an experts' opinions gives your work credibility. There is a serious problem, however, when you use somebody else's material – their **intellectual property** – without their permission or without referring to it as being theirs. This is known as a **breach of copyright** and is a form of property theft.

Intellectual property is something that you have created: for example a book, a song, a computer program, a product or a brand name. **Copyright** is your right of ownership to that property, to reproduce it and to receive an income from it. It is shown by the © symbol.

If you are going to use someone else's work by repeating what they have said, either by directly quoting them or by rewording what they have said, then you should make it clear that you are using their work. Using someone else's work without saying so is known as **plagiarism**.

Plagiarism is seen as dishonest – when you are plagiarising, you are presenting someone else's work as your own. You do not have to be directly copying to be plagiarising. If you re-word what is said by someone else and present it as your own work then that is also plagiarising. It is not only wrong to use someone else's words, it is also wrong to use their ideas.

where to find the reference data in a book

The normal place to find all the information for a reference in a printed book is the second page, ie on the back of the title page. The illustration below shows the relevant page in an Osborne Books textbook 'Working in Accounting and Finance Tutorial'. A reference for a quotation on page 30 of this book this will therefore be:

(Working in Accounting and Finance Tutorial, M. Fardon, 2013, p30.)

The title, of course, is printed on the title page.

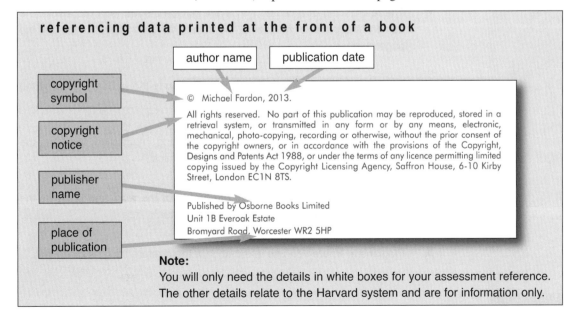

referencing data printed at the front of a book

author name   publication date

copyright symbol

copyright notice

publisher name

place of publication

© Michael Fardon, 2013.

All rights reserved. No part of this publication may be reproduced, stored in a retrieval system, or transmitted in any form or by any means, electronic, mechanical, photo-copying, recording or otherwise, without the prior consent of the copyright owners, or in accordance with the provisions of the Copyright, Designs and Patents Act 1988, or under the terms of any licence permitting limited copying issued by the Copyright Licensing Agency, Saffron House, 6-10 Kirby Street, London EC1N 8TS.

Published by Osborne Books Limited
Unit 1B Everoak Estate
Bromyard Road, Worcester WR2 5HP

Note:
You will only need the details in white boxes for your assessment reference.
The other details relate to the Harvard system and are for information only.

Chapter Summary

- Information must be located, extracted and stored to be ready for use.

- You must make sure that you are able to reference information and be able to find it again for checking.

- Information may be paper-based, electronic or sourced through people that you know.

- You must check that information is reliable and accurate.

- Checking the same information with two or more sources is called triangulation.

- Care must be taken when looking at survey results.

- Information must be relevant to your needs, for example tax information must be for the correct country and tax year.

- Storing information in an organised way, whether on paper or electronically, will help to save time retrieving the information when you need it.

- The referencing of information from books will include the title, author(s), the date of publication and the page number.

- The referencing of a written article will include the name of the article, the name of the paper or magazine, the author, the date of publication and the page number.

- The referencing of electronic sources will include the webpage link and the date that you accessed the information.

- There are more formal methods of referencing information, including the Harvard Referencing system used by academics.

- Good referencing gives credit to the author of the work and respects the intellectual property and copyright of the author.

- Plagiarism, where you use information without referencing, is dishonest.

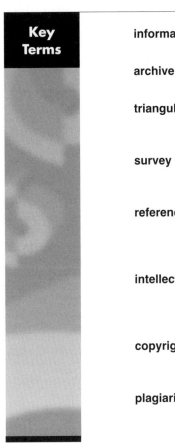

Key Terms

information source	the place or book where information is found
archive records	stored records and documents, no longer in use
triangulation	where you cross check information with at least two independent sources to see if it is correct
survey	where a number of people are asked a question or series of questions, often about their opinions
referencing	giving credit in your work to the author of the work you are quoting or from whom you get the ideas – it also allows information to be retrieved and checked
intellectual property	something created by a person – for example a book, a song, a computer program, a brand name – which then becomes that person's property
copyright	the name given to the legal right of ownership of intellectual property
plagiarism	using someone else's work without saying so – it is seen as dishonest

Activities

Tick the correct answers for each question.

Note that there may be more than one correct answer to a question.

5.1   The order of the main stages of sourcing information are: ✔

(a)	Extracting, storing and locating information	
(b)	Locating, extracting and storing information	
(c)	Locating, storing and extracting information	

5.2   The sources of information listed in the left-hand column of the table below can be sorted into one or more categories: paper-based, digital and people.

Tick the appropriate boxes in the three columns on the right.

Source of information	Paper-based ✔	Digital ✔	People ✔
Books			
Family			
Magazines			
Archives			
Manager			
Search engines			
Visiting speaker			
Journals			
Webinar			
Teacher			

5.3 Sheila is going to the library, what will she find there to provide her with information?

✔

(a)	Computers	
(b)	Books	
(c)	Magazines	
(d)	Archives	
(e)	Library staff	

5.4 Published information is always correct.

✔

(a)	True	
(b)	False	

5.5 Phoebe thinks that some information she has sourced may be incorrect. The source seems to be reliable but Phoebe wants to check with another source. What is the term used to describe the process of checking two or more sources to prove the reliability of information?

Enter the answer in the box below.

5.6 Amil is reviewing a survey that was carried out by a business that he is researching.

The marketing department of the business wrote the survey questions and then sent them out to existing customers. How do you think Amil should view the reliability of the results of the survey?

Tick the factors below which will enable Amir to confirm the reliability of the survey.

✔

(a)	The results will be reliable as 1,000 customers were surveyed	
(b)	The questions may need to be reviewed to make sure that they are fair questions	
(c)	Amil can trust the survey because the marketing department wrote the questions	

5.7 Information found by asking a question through a search engine online is always relevant to your project.

✔

(a)	True	
(b)	False	

5.8 Amil needs to save the information about the business that he is studying for his AAT qualification. What will be the best way to manage his computer files?

✔

(a)	Have a folder for each AAT unit and put everything into it	
(b)	Have a single folder for all his AAT studies	
(c)	Have a folder for each AAT unit and a sub folder for each topic or section of the unit	

5.9 Calum is keeping his information on paper. What is the best way to organise his information?

✔

(a)	Keep everything in his bag	
(b)	Have a folder for each unit and dividers for each topic	
(c)	Keep everything in a big box at home	

5.10 Sandra is referencing an article that she found in the AAT magazine. What does she need to include in the reference using the simple referencing method (not the Harvard method).

✔

(a)	Magazine title, author name, publication date, page number of article	
(b)	Magazine publisher, author name, publication date, place of publication	
(c)	Magazine title, author name, place of publication, page number of article	

5.11   Sonia is referencing a web-based article. What does she need to include in the reference using the simple referencing method (not the Harvard method).

✔

(a)	The name of the webpage and the author of the article	
(b)	The link to the webpage and the date the page was accessed	
(c)	The link to the webpage and the date the data was posted to the website	

5.12   An example of intellectual property is:

✔

(a)	A library	
(b)	The brand name of a series of books	
(c)	An email to a colleague	

5.13   Making unauthorised CDs of practice exam questions from a publisher's website is best described as:

✔

(a)	A breach of copyright	
(b)	Referencing	
(c)	Creating intellectual property	

5.14   Jamie has decided to reword an idea from his textbook so that he does not have to reference it. This is known as 'plagiarism'.

✔

(a)	True	
(b)	False	

6 Taking notes

this chapter covers...

This chapter describes in detail the many different ways of taking notes as part of your studies and how best to organise them. The chapter includes the following:

■ *an overview of different methods of note taking*

■ *how to use notes to help you revise and memorise your learning*

■ *how to decide what to note*

■ *bullet point note taking*

■ *electronic notes*

■ *refining your notes*

■ *organising your notes*

■ *using flow diagrams*

■ *using spray diagrams*

■ *structured note taking – using tables to present information*

■ *the process of embedding learning in your long-term memory*

THE PROCESSES OF TAKING NOTES

different types of notes – an overview

If you are able to take accurate, meaningful notes you will improve your learning and your chances of success in your assessments.

Note taking is done at different times during your course:

- **the first stage of learning** – writing down the important points when listening to a teacher, taking notes from a book, listening to an audio recording

- **refining the notes** – this follows the first stage and organises and summarises the notes gathered in the first stage, using techniques such as lists of points, structured tables, spray diagrams and flow diagrams

- **transferring information into long-term memory** – rereading the summarised material (notes, diagrams etc) and developing them further into learning aids such as posters involving text and diagrams, index cards, audio recordings – the object here is to embed the information into your long-term memory

Many of these activities can be carried out on paper, but increasingly electronic devices can be used to produce the learning material.

Study the diagram below which summarises these three processes.

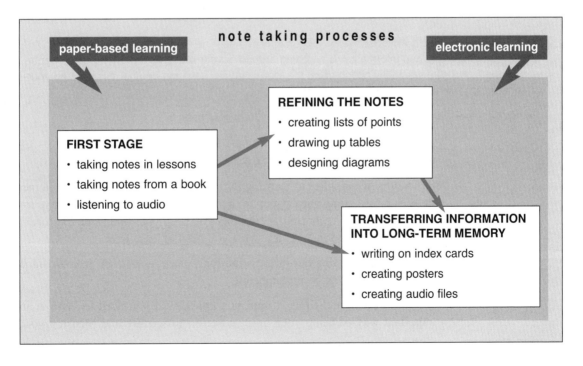

different types of notes – what suits you?

As you will see from the last page, note taking is a method of recording information. Different people use different methods. It is part of your learning process to discover which methods suits you best.

Before investigating the different note taking methods you can use, you need to understand how your brain deals with the information when it receives it.

TAKING NOTES – OFFLOADING FROM YOUR BRAIN

why you need to offload

You cannot remember everything immediately and all at once. Writing things down **offloads information** out of your brain, giving your brain a chance to concentrate on receiving and processing new information.

Example:

Exam panic – brain overload problem

If you have ever had a panic before you go into an exam and cause yourself more stress by thinking: 'I must remember all these facts and theories' then you are likely to forget the facts and theories.

Avoid brain overload

Make sure that you learn as you do the course, do not think 'I'll revise that for the exam'. Putting skills and information into your long-term memory reduces exam panic.

Dump information from your brain

If you are in the exam and information is whizzing around in your brain, ask for some scrap paper and spend 1 or 2 minutes briefly noting down the ideas that are hovering around, this will free your brain to get on with answering the exam questions.

Remember: writing things down **offloads information** from your brain.

when you need to offload

Offloading also applies to learning in the classroom, in the library, at home. Putting information onto paper or into some other external memory, for example an audio recording, means that you keep your brain free to process new ideas. You can then review what you need to learn later.

When you are finding out information for a piece of work or project, much of it will not need to be remembered.

Writing it down and filing it until you know what you need to learn is an important way of using your time and effort efficiently and focusing your efforts.

STAGE ONE: KEY WORDS, TRIGGER WORDS, BULLET LISTS

to note or not to note?

There are many situations where you will need to take notes. Taking notes is a useful way to help you to remember information – the process can make passive learning situations **active** rather than **passive**, and far more effective.

When you are in a lecture, it is tempting to write down everything that your teacher says, but you should avoid this. Writing so much so quickly will distract you from what your teacher is saying and may prevent you from understanding it. On the other hand if you write nothing down and hope that you will remember it later it is likely that you will forget it.

So you cannot win – no note taking and you may forget everything that was said – write too much and you might miss the point. There are, fortunately, various situations and techniques which will enable you to write down what you need to learn when the information is coming at you at a fast rate.

knowing when you need to take notes

There are a number of classroom situations when you will know that you have to take notes:

■ When the teacher writes notes **on the board** or presents you with a **slide**.

You should summarise everything as the teacher writes it on the board or explains the slide. If something is important enough to give you in note form, it is important enough for you to copy it down.

■ When the teacher includes **key words** in what he or she is saying.

A **key word** is the important one – the word or words that sum up what is being said. Whether you are taking notes from written text, lectures, podcasts or videos, you should listen out for key words.

■ When the teacher includes **trigger words** in what he or she is saying.

Trigger words and phrases are words or phrases that come before important information. When you are taking notes, look out for **trigger words** and phrases from your teacher. You should note down everything that comes after trigger words because it is important.

Here are some examples of trigger words:

– *importantly* . . .

– *you need to remember that* . . .

– *finally* . . .

– *note that* . . .

– *in the exam* . . .

We will now look at a range of useful note taking methods. Learners should experiment with each type to find out which suits their style best or which works for the different study situations in which they find themselves.

bullet point lists

A bullet point list is a series of short phrases and sentences, or even words, set out on individual lines, preceded by a bullet point like this '•'.

This last sentence could be set out much more clearly like this:

> A bullet point list is:
>
> • A series of short phrases and sentences, or even just words
>
> • Set out on individual lines
>
> • Preceded by a bullet point like this '·'

This makes it far easier to understand as the reader can take in each line as a new piece of information.

using bullet points to summarise

The bullet point list shown above simply chops up the sentence into meaningful bits, but it has not reduced the number of words to read.

A bullet point list can also be used **to summarise text or words spoken** by a teacher. This is the real skill of note taking – reducing the number of words you have to write without losing any of the meaning or detail.

For example, the explanatory text on the previous page could be summarised in bullet point form as follows:

> • Taking notes – useful tool to learning – passive to active
>
> • If everything written down – difficult to remember information
>
> • No notes written – forget, too much to remember – miss point
>
> • Copy from board or slide if information given by teacher
>
> • Identify key words – they sum up the main points
>
> • Look out for trigger words – useful points will follow

In the above example of note taking using a bulleted list, 363 words of written text have been reduced to a total of only 55 words.

electronic notes

The increased use of mobile phones, tablets and other electronic devices means that both visual and textual information can now be easily captured and saved, for example by copying and pasting text from a useful website.

Even though it is easy to obtain a lot of information quickly this way it is really important that you have taken it in and learnt from it, not just saved it without reading the useful parts thoroughly. Examples of note taking involving electronic devices include the following:

■ slides

Your lecturer will usually give you copies of slides shown on the whiteboard. If you have a paper copy before the presentation then you can make notes next to the slides when they are shown. The example below is taken from a slide presentation of 'Balancing double-entry accounts'.

Note that the student has added a way of remembering that 'c/d' (carried down) is entered above the total and 'b/d' (brought down) is entered below the total: when you think of clothing 'cap' is always at the top and 'boots' are on your feet (at the bottom). This was probably said by the teacher.

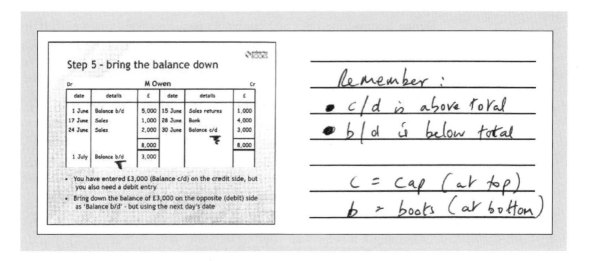

■ smart boards

Some smart boards allow the teacher to save or export what is presented onscreen as a PowerPoint or pdf file. Both of these formats can be emailed or uploaded onto learning platforms for students to access.

This means that you need not copy what is written on them but can make notes on them when you have accessed them.

- **snapping on a mobile phone**

Some teachers may be happy to allow students to photograph what has been written on flipchart paper or whiteboards so that they can makes notes later on. You must always ask permission before taking photographs.

- **making an audio recording of a lesson**

You may also be able to sound record lessons and make notes later, although some teachers will not allow live recordings. Again, you should always ask permission before you do make a recording.

- **making notes from research on the internet**

If you are researching through books or on the internet, you can record your notes electronically either by saving pages from the screen (making sure that you can reference them), or by making an audio recording of your thoughts on your phone or other recording device.

STAGE TWO – WRITING UP AND REFINING YOUR NOTES

why write up your notes?

During lectures, meetings and other note taking sessions you are likely to take rough notes, abbreviated (key word) notes or bullet point lists. As soon as you can you must go through these notes and make sure that they make sense by writing them out more fully. This is an important process because:

- if you do not write up your notes you may find that in a few weeks your notes make no sense at all

- writing something down makes it more likely that you will remember it and so re-writing your notes out longhand and rewording your notes makes it even more likely that you will remember – this is a good example of active learning and a very successful strategy

- going through your notes at the end of each day re-enforces your learning – it helps with your organisation of the information; if you do this at the end of each session it will refresh your memory and will make sure that the writing up task does not get too big or take too long

Top tip: Ever thought 'I'll remember'? Treat it as an alarm. If you think 'I'll remember' then that is your brain saying – 'NO You won't remember!' Make sure that you write out the necessary information in full with a good explanation because if you do not then you may find that you have forgotten something important.

Self-discipline is key!

organising your notes

Spending a little time making sure that your notes are organised will save you a lot of time later when you come to revise and prepare for an assessment. This will also help you later on if you need to refer back to the subject, perhaps on your next level of course.

Good organisational skills are also valuable in the workplace: employers value staff who are able to organise themselves and are impressed by employees who can access notes and documents quickly.

Organisation of your notes requires you to be logical and to choose the methods which you find most effective. This topic was briefly covered in the last chapter (page 73), but here are some more ideas to help:

- **large ring binders** or **concertina files** to collect your notes for each subject you study (eg 'Developing Study Skills') – these can be subdivided into individual topics (eg 'Taking Notes') using card dividers in the case of ring binders and the pockets provided in a concertina file

- if you are using large ring binders it can be useful to use different **coloured paper** for different topics or types of notes

- if you are using ring binders or concertina files, remember to **file your notes** at the end of a study session, otherwise they may get lost

- **notebooks** for individual subjects or for individual topics which you can write up as the 'second version' of your original notes, entries in these notebooks should be headed up clearly and dated so that material can easily be accessed by flicking through the note book

- **index cards** for individual parts of topics which can be used to record definitions, formulas, calculations – these are also very helpful for revision

Note that:

- there is no overall 'best' way to organise notes; the best way is the way that best suits you personally

- putting together notes as you progress through the individual topics – this enables you to produce your own personal 'textbook' which will help you both learn and revise

- the suggestions listed on this page can be adapted for use on computers and other electronic devices

FURTHER TECHNIQUES FOR PRESENTING INFORMATION

So far in this chapter we have described how you should record and organise your notes. This has involved two stages:

■ the first stage – making your first basic notes

■ the second stage – rewriting and refining your first basic notes

During the second stage, which refines your notes and helps to embed the information in your long-term memory, you may choose to use one of the following methods:

■ **flow diagrams** – which shows a process taking place, stage by stage

■ **spray diagrams** (also known as spider diagrams, tree diagrams, mind maps, concept maps) – which show how the various elements of your learning tie up together and relate to each other

■ **structured notes** – ie setting out the information in logical tables

We will deal with each of these in turn.

flow diagrams

A flow diagram shows a series of activities taking place over time

Flow diagrams (also known as 'flow charts') are used to illustrate the stages of a process. They can also be developed and used for project planning, but for your notes the simple form will be the most useful. Here is part of an example from the last chapter (page 67) used to shown the process of extracting and using information.

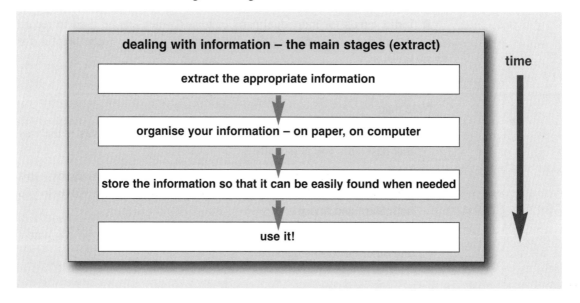

Note that the individual boxes in the diagram:

■ are arranged in time order – in this case starting at the top

■ are linked by arrows pointing in the direction of the order that the separate operations are carried out

■ are clearly described in short simple terms

If you are technically minded and would like to present a flow chart in a professional way you will find that Microsoft Word has tools which you can use to construct them on your computer.

spray diagrams

A spray diagram shows how the various elements of learning relate to each other

Spray diagrams – also known as spider diagrams, tree diagrams, mind maps and concept maps – are a **visual way** of organising information and concepts. Spray diagrams are used to:

■ take notes

■ think through an issue that you encounter

■ think through a topic that you need to learn about

■ organise facts, issues or ideas into a structured form

They should be as simple as possible. You can add colour by highlighting or using coloured pens to indicate different categories of information.

The example below shows how you could draw a spray diagram on the topic of 'double-entry bookkeeping'.

Note how the diagram gradually builds up. You start with the main topic in the middle of the page which then 'sprays' out to link to other topic headings, usually circled. From each topic heading you add notes which sometimes lead onto other notes.

Example:

Creating a spray diagram

Step 1: start with the main topic in the centre, within an oval

double-entry bookkeeping

Step 2: add related sub-topics in similar ovals, connected by lines to the main subject

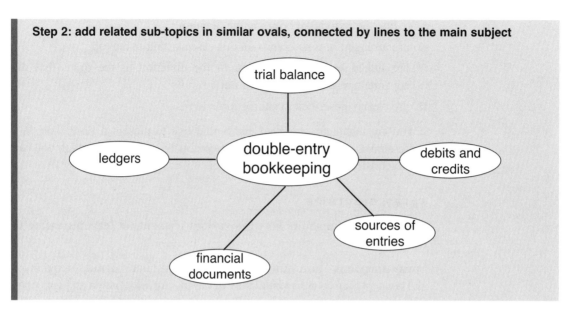

Step 3: now add notes to the new sub-topics, connected by lines to the new sub-topic

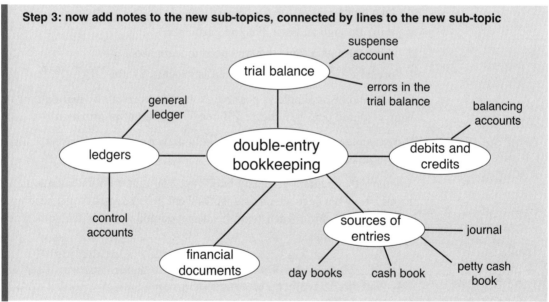

Note the following:

■ the main topic and related sub-topics are in ovals

■ the notes in Step 3 are in text only, not in ovals, and could be added to as you think of extra notes and links that relate to each other

■ if you add notes to notes, they should be linked by further lines – eg you could add types of control account, day books or financial documents

■ because the spray diagram is a visual representation of the topic showing how each sub-topic links to the others it may be more easily memorised than a long block of text

structured notes - using tables

You may decide to set up structured notes, eg in the form of a table where the first column and headings are completed and you fill in the rest. The table below shows the features of various types of note taking and will help you to decide on the best way of gathering information for a particular project.

Note taking method	Advantages	Disadvantages
Key words	*Short and easy to write. Keeps the brain free enough to process what is being read or said. Active learning as you have to identify the key words.*	*Must be neatly written and clear enough for you to understand later.*
Bulleted lists	*Organised layout, it is easy to follow and for you to find what has been said. Active learning as you have to identify the bullets.*	*Might be difficult for you to go back to something said earlier and add to the notes.*
Audio recording	*Little effort required. Allows you to get a full recording while still taking key word or similar notes to keep the learning active.*	*It may be hard to find specific points that are in the middle of the recording. You must have permission. Only passive learning if you simply listen.*
Photograph of flip charts or whiteboard	*Little effort, an exact copy of what the teacher has written and allows you to listen and take key word notes to make the learning active.*	*Must have permission. Passive learning if you do not take notes and just listen.*
Structured notes (tables)	*Organised layout and will help you to make sure that you find specific information that you need for a project. Can be active as you are looking to identify key information to fit into the table.*	*May be restrictive as you focus only on what you have decided that you need. Lack of space prevents you from recording extra useful information you might find later on.*
Spray diagrams	*Appeals to visual learners. Can be adapted and used with other note taking techniques. Can show links in ways that bullet list cannot show. Very Active as you identify key words and make connections.*	*Linking lines and relationships between topics must be clear enough for you to be able to understand them later on.*

EMBEDDING INFORMATION INTO LONG-TERM MEMORY

So far in this chapter we have described the first two stages of note taking:

■ the **first stage** – making your first basic notes

■ the **second stage** – rewriting and refining your first basic notes

The second part of the note taking process, where you refine your notes, will help you to understand the information and help to **embed the information** into your **long-term memory**.

The **third stage** of note taking also involves **embedding information.**

Here are some **hints on embedding**:

■ to help you to embed information you need to actively engage with your notes by making posters, quizzes, memory cards or simply putting notices around your house – this will help you embed the **Knowledge** sections of the accounting qualification

■ for the **Skills** sections of the qualification you should make sure that you practise problem-solving questions and scenario questions, using your notes to help you

■ take advantage of all the online resources available to you which were described in Chapter 4 (see pages 56-59), for example interactive practice questions and crosswords

doing the 'right' work

To make the most of your time you should always make sure you are '**doing the right work**'.

As we saw in Chapter 1, many students are often tempted to leave until the end the topics that they find difficult or dislike. As a result they may not spend enough time on the areas where work will benefit them the most.

When you decide what to study, make sure that you spend more time on the topics that you find most challenging and the areas which you do not like or find boring.

You are not 'working smart' if you spend too much time making your notes look attractive. This may be fun and you might enjoy it, but you need to spend your time productively looking at a topic you do not fully understand yet.

Another good use of your time and energy is to practise questions in areas you find challenging, repeating quizzes or test papers where you have not yet got all the answers correct.

Chapter Summary

- Note taking has three stages:
  - your initial notes taken in class or when studying
  - refining and organising your notes to put them into a usable order
  - embedding the information from your notes into your long-term memory

- Different people use different methods of note taking – and will normally use the method that suits them best.

- You can dump information from your short-term memory onto paper to free your brain to solve problems.

- You will not need to know all the information that you research – keeping notes in an organised way saves you from memorising everything.

- You can use bulleted notes – summarising what is said – to cut down on the amount of writing you have to do.

- Look for key phrases and trigger words that your tutor uses such as 'it's really important that...' This will guide you in what to note down.

- Electronic notes given to you, such as a teacher's slides, can save you having to write them down, but you must review them and interact with them for learning to be effective.

- You should ask permission from your teacher to make an audio recording or to photograph the board.

- Writing up your notes straightaway is important – in a week or so you may not remember enough about the lesson to understand the notes.

- You can organise your notes in whatever way suits you – so long as the notes are organised in an efficient way.

- Flow diagrams are useful for showing a process that happens in several steps, such as a calculation.

- Spray diagrams are very visual and useful in illustrating links between concepts.

- Structured notes can help to organise research for a project or can simply be used to organise what you have learned.

- You should embed knowledge and learn skills as you go along – it will make exams and later learning easier.

refining notes	an activity where you take your initial notes and check and rewrite them, making sure that they make sense and will be useful for revision
embedding information	a process where you make sure that you have transferred information from your short-term memory to your long-term memory
offloading	a process where you 'dump' information from your short-term memory onto paper to free your brain to process more information and problems
bulleted lists	a way of writing summarised notes after bullet points, for example the chapter summary on the previous page
key words	important words that summarise or describe what is being discussed, for example: 'many situations, take notes, remember information, active rather than passive, effective' – note that 'key *words*' should not be confused with the 'key *terms*' on this page which are technical definitions
trigger words or phrases	important words or phrases that your teacher uses to alert you to important information, for example: 'importantly', 'remember that'
electronic notes	notes that are saved and stored electronically, eg on computer – examples might be your own notes or your lecturer's slides or Smart board summaries
flow diagrams	a diagram that shows a series of tasks in the order in which they are completed
spray diagrams	a visual way of organising information, showing how concepts and ideas to be learned link together
structured notes	using tables to list what you need to find out or to organise what you have found out

Activities

Tick the correct answers for each question.

Note that there may be more than one correct answer to a question.

6.1   Taking notes in class (choose one option): ✔

(a)	Is a form of passive learning	
(b)	Is a form of refining notes	
(c)	Provides a resource to help with studying	

6.2   The first stage of note taking is (choose all the correct answers): ✔

(a)	When you make notes on what the teacher is saying	
(b)	When you make notes on what you are looking at in a book or on screen	
(c)	When you save Web pages or electronic slides to look at later	

6.3   Sheila is listening for trigger words to help her to take notes. A trigger word is (choose one option): ✔

(a)	A word that is said very quickly and could be missed	
(b)	A word that comes before important information	
(c)	A word that summarises important information	

6.4   Sam is using bullet points to help her to take notes. The main advantage of using bullet points is: ✔

(a)	They save you having to remember all the important points in a lesson	
(b)	You can then read and understand the main lesson points more easily	

6.5   The second stage of note taking is (choose the correct answers):   ✔

(a)	Reviewing and tidying up your initial notes	
(b)	Making an audio recording of a lesson	
(c)	A stage which helps you understand and remember the main points	

6.6   Picking out the key words will help you to identify important parts of the lesson.   ✔

(a)	True	
(b)	False	

6.7   Aurora is experimenting with note taking. Her friend, Adam, has told her that she should always use spray diagrams but she isn't sure about this. A spray diagram is useful for (choose one option):   ✔

(a)	Showing a series of activities over a period of time	
(b)	Showing how concepts and facts to be learned link together	
(c)	Explaining how a specific process works	

6.8   Aseem favours the use of flow diagrams. A flow diagram is used for (choose one option):   ✔

(a)	Showing the stages of a process which involves several steps	
(b)	Highlighting the items that need to be offloaded from short-term memory	
(c)	Summarising the main points of a lesson	

6.9   The advantages of structured note taking are (choose the correct answers):   ✔

(a)	It helps you to focus on what information you need to find	
(b)	It is useful for comparisons like advantages and disadvantages	
(c)	The layout is organised, making it easy to see information	
(d)	It shows how concepts can be linked together	

6.10   The third stage of note taking involves (choose the correct answers):   ✔

(a)	Using your notes to learn the knowledge parts of the syllabus	
(b)	Using your notes to help practise the skills parts of the syllabus	
(c)	Watching videos relating to the topics you are studying	

6.11   Put each of the words or phrases which are shown below in bold type in the appropriate space in the right-hand column of the table – ie against the correct description.

Key terms   Structured notes   Key words   Refining notes   Embedding information

Flow diagrams   Trigger words   Offloading

(a)	Ensuring your learning moves to your long-term memory	
(b)	Words that let you know that something important is coming	
(c)	Technical words or phrases	
(d)	A formal table or list which organises your research or notes	
(e)	The process of dumping information from your brain to free it up for taking in new information and ideas	
(f)	Tidying and making sense of your notes	
(g)	A diagram setting out the stages of a process	
(h)	Words which summarise or describe what is being said	

7 Writing the Action Plan

this chapter covers...

This chapter explains how to set up the Action Plan that you will need in order to plan the set piece of work which forms part of your assessment.

You will learn in this chapter:

- *that your set piece can be chosen from a range of topics and agreed with your tutor*

- *your set piece can be presented in a number of different ways – for example a written project or a presentation – also to be agreed with your tutor*

- *that you will need an Action Plan to plan your set piece*

- *how to lay out your Action Plan in columns*

- *what the columns are for*

- *the types of entries made in the Action Plan – for example making a list of tasks to complete*

- *that your entries in your Action Plan must be in the right order with enough information to make them clear*

- *that the content of your Action Plan will be used as evidence in your assessment*

PLANNING YOUR SET PIECE OF WORK

deciding on the set piece of work

A large part of this unit is taken up by the need to action plan and complete a **set piece of work** which you will present to your assessor.

The piece of work can be any **one** of the following:

- form part of the work of any Unit in the AAT Level 2 Diploma in Accounting and Business where tutor feedback is allowed

- be a research project on accounting or business

- be about your own personal development, eg a CV

- be about a different topic which will demonstrate the development of your presentational skills

The **format** of the piece of work can be:

- a presentation to an individual or group using presentation software

- a verbal presentation of a piece of work not involving software

- a written report or essay

- any combination of methods of presentation

the planning process

In order to complete and present your set piece of work you will need to plan what you are going to do by following these four stages:

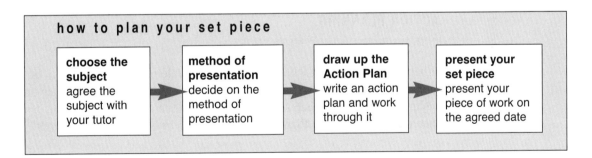

how to plan your set piece

| **choose the subject** agree the subject with your tutor | **method of presentation** decide on the method of presentation | **draw up the Action Plan** write an action plan and work through it | **present your set piece** present your piece of work on the agreed date |

discussing your set piece with your assessor

You have seen that you have a range of choices about the topic and style of presentation of your piece of work. This is because you are being assessed on the following:

- the plan that you use to produce your piece of work – your Action Plan
- receiving feedback on your plan and/or work
- making changes based on the feedback
- describing how your plan and your set piece of work has improved because of the feedback

The work that you produce for assessment is important, so you need to produce it to a good standard.

tutor involvement in your set piece

It may be that your tutor/assessor wants to advise you about the topic of your set piece of work. It may be that the tutor/assessor wants to keep your workload to a minimum. On the other hand your tutor may advise you to focus on a certain topic to strengthen your knowledge and skills or increase your learning in that area.

Whether or not you are given a set piece of work or allowed to suggest your own, you should clearly agree the following points with your tutor:

- the topic, including the depth/detail required
- how the set piece is to be presented
- the length of your piece of work (eg word count or length of presentation)
- how many information sources you should use and reference
- the final completion date
- the date by which you should complete each stage of the set piece – these are known as 'milestones' and will include dates for handing in your work in order to get tutor feedback

ACTION PLANNING

When you have agreed with your tutor a schedule of what you need to do, you should break the work into small tasks. You should then decide a date on which you will finish each small task or 'milestone' along the way. You can then draw up an Action Plan, which should also be agreed with your tutor.

why do you need an Action Plan?

An Action Plan is a list of tasks that need to be done in order to complete a project.

The simplest Action Plan is a 'to do' list which lists the things you need to do so that you do not have to remember them. A 'to do' list can be very simple but also very effective, as seen in the example on the next page.

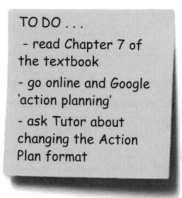

Writing down the tasks that you need to complete, like writing things to do on a post-it note, frees the brain to get on with whatever you need to do. The effect of this is that:

■ tasks or their hand-in date do not need to be remembered

■ not needing to remember unclutters your short-term memory

■ uncluttering allows your brain to work on other problems

The same principle applies to a more **formal extended Action Plan** which will be required for an extended project – such as your set piece. This type of Action Plan will enable you to understand:

■ what needs to be done

■ when it needs to be done

Agreeing deadlines ('milestones') – ie dates by which tasks need to be completed – has the following benefits:

■ it stops tasks from drifting – this is where tasks take much longer than they should because there seems to be no urgency

■ it stops tasks from piling up, making the project feel overwhelming

the importance of avoiding wasting time

You may find that a task will take as long as you have to complete it. If you only have an hour then you will do it in that hour, if you have three days then you may put it off, think about it, avoid it and then do it at the last minute.

Alternatively you may start the task and take a long time to complete it because you want to do it just right and you keep changing what you have done until you run out of time.

Both of these approaches are **a potential waste of time and effort**. Careful planning will help you avoid these situations.

HOW TO PLAN

You will need three important pieces of information to make your plan:

■ the required completion date

■ an outline of what needs to be done

■ an estimate of how much time you have available to do the project

Once you have these three pieces of information then you need to look at the outline of what needs to be done and break it down into manageable tasks.

You will then need to:

■ make a list of the individual tasks and decide how long each task is likely to take

■ identify any help and resources that you need for each task

■ list the identified tasks in an order that will allow you to complete them all before the required completion date

■ write out your Action Plan, including all the projected dates for completion of the tasks

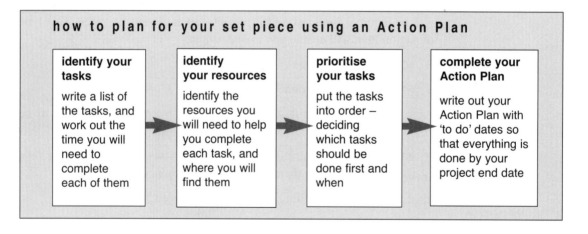

how to plan for your set piece using an Action Plan

identify your tasks	identify your resources	prioritise your tasks	complete your Action Plan
write a list of the tasks, and work out the time you will need to complete each of them	identify the resources you will need to help you complete each task, and where you will find them	put the tasks into order – deciding which tasks should be done first and when	write out your Action Plan with 'to do' dates so that everything is done by your project end date

ACTION PLAN FORMAT

It is recommended that you use a table to record your Action Plan.

The AAT suggests that you use the type of table shown on the next page. This is a useful format for an Action Plan for your set piece, although you can alter it and add to it as you think is necessary.

If you do make any changes to the format, make sure that you agree them with your tutor as you will be assessed on your Action Plan.

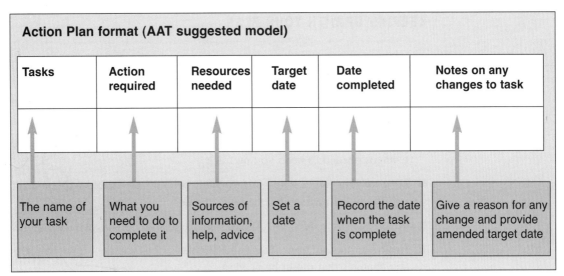

Action Plan format (AAT suggested model)

Tasks	Action required	Resources needed	Target date	Date completed	Notes on any changes to task
The name of your task	What you need to do to complete it	Sources of information, help, advice	Set a date	Record the date when the task is complete	Give a reason for any change and provide amended target date

Your Action Plan also sets out:

■ the way in which the set piece of work will be presented, with an explanation of why the presentation method has been chosen (see Chapter 9 for presentation methods)

■ the process of monitoring the project (target date compared with date completed)

■ any changes to the plan and reasons for the changes made

Set out below is an extract – with sample entries – from an Action Plan for a set piece on the topic of Value Added Tax (VAT).

Project Action Plan – the UK VAT system (extract)

Tasks	Action required	Resources needed	Target date	Date completed	Notes on any changes to task
Find out about UK VAT rates	Find two examples of two different UK VAT rates and the items they are charged on	Internet access to HMRC website (computer room)	3 March	5 March	Computers all booked on 3 March. Booked for 5 March instead
Get pictures for slides	Get pictures of VAT-able items identified in the last task	Computer screen-grabs, or camera on mobile	10 March		

KEEPING UP WITH YOUR PLAN

keeping your plan on target

It is important that you keep your plan well on target. Writing an Action Plan is one thing, but keeping to it is another. You will need to:

■ set review dates when you will look over your plan and make any changes needed to keep you on track

■ keep to your target dates – if you fall behind you should explain your reasons in the notes and set a revised date

■ build spare time into your Action Plan to deal with unexpected problems

■ finish well before your final hand-in date so that you have time to make any changes that might be needed

doing your tasks in the right order

As part of your planning, you need to decide the order in which you should complete your tasks. You will need to bear in mind that:

■ some tasks must be done before others

■ some tasks will be more urgent than others

■ some tasks will take a long time to complete

■ the completion of some tasks will not depend on you finishing other tasks, so these can be done more or less at any time

■ research must come before writing and presenting

■ you may have to wait for other people to give you information

■ you may have to book the use of specialist equipment, for example the use of a projector to practise or to give a presentation

a tip for sorting out the tasks

One way of planning the order of your tasks is to write down the name of each task and the estimated time it will take:

■ on separate pieces of paper, or

■ on the computer, eg as a simple list with each task on a new line

You should then:

■ move ('shuffle') the tasks around on a table or on the computer screen and sort them in the order which you think is best

■ allocate each task a consecutive number and write it by the task name

You can then arrange the tasks on a 'time line' which will form the basis of your Action Plan. This process (which, by the way, is a good example of kinesthetic learning) is shown in the diagram below.

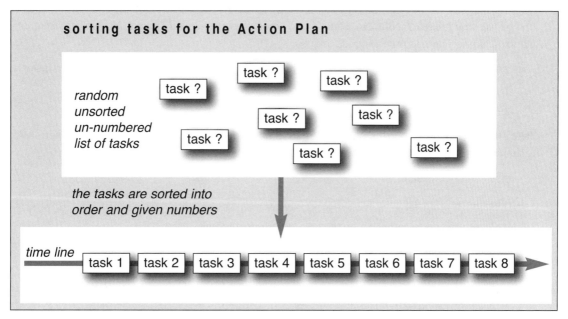

sorting tasks for the Action Plan

random unsorted un-numbered list of tasks

task ?   task ?   task ?   task ?   task ?   task ?   task ?   task ?

the tasks are sorted into order and given numbers

time line   task 1   task 2   task 3   task 4   task 5   task 6   task 7   task 8

under-planning – why is it a problem?

'Under-planning' simply means 'not doing enough planning'.

It is always helpful to break project tasks into small 'chunks' so that each task does not get too big. For example, if you give a task a name like 'research information' this does not give much detail about how and what to research for this large task, and so it will be difficult for you to estimate how much time it will take to complete it.

When you are planning you should:

■ make sure that you have enough detail so that nothing is missed; if you have to research, you must be clear about what information is needed

■ make sure that you break major tasks into manageable smaller tasks

■ put enough detail into the 'Action required' column to help you to decide how long a task will take

If you cannot estimate how much time something will take, then your Action Plan will not be accurate. 'Under-planning' may:

■ use up more time in the long run as you waste time looking at the wrong things or doing the wrong things

■ mean that you have to go back to an earlier task and do it again because it was not done correctly in the first place

Example:

Jake's Project: Trevaan Harnesses

Jake is interested in mountaineering and mountain safety equipment. He has agreed with his tutor that he will do a presentation about a safety equipment business called Trevaan Harnesses. Jake is planning to analyse their marketing techniques.

Jake agreed a date for the presentation and started to write his Action Plan. It contained only two tasks:

1   research the company (one week)

2   write the presentation (two weeks)

Jake's tutor gave him feedback saying that Jake needed much more detail, so Jake divided the research task (task 1) into two separate tasks:

·   research advertisements

·   research selling outlets for the company's products

He also divided the presentation task (task 2) into three separate tasks:

·   design the slides

·   write the presentation

·   set up the presentation

But Jake then ran into further problems:

1   Jake's Action Plan does not give him enough detail about researching the advertisements: he will need to look at television and radio, newspapers and magazines, online advertising, the company website and company social media. He is in danger of not covering enough types of advertising. These should be itemised in the plan.

2   Jake is planning to research the selling outlets used by the company. But what is he going to be investigating – is he just going to list them or is he going to discuss pricing, discounts and offers? Again, these should be itemised in the plan.

3   What about the writing of the presentation? Jake could break down the writing of the presentation into sections about printed advertising, online advertising and should design the colour and layout of the slides after writing the presentation. Again, these should be itemised in the plan.

Conclusion:

An Action Plan needs enough detail to make sure a project can be correctly scheduled and then monitored efficiently. If changes need to be made or the schedule needs to be revised because of problems or delays, the plan can be updated and the tasks completed successfully.

over-planning – why is it also a problem?

'Over-planning' simply means 'doing too much planning'.

You can see from the above example that under-planning is a problem because you may not do enough preparation or you may not focus on the tasks that need to be completed most urgently.

Over-planning is also a problem because:

■ too much time is spent planning which reduces the working time

■ making sure you have planned every last, tiny detail might mean that your plan is not flexible enough to allow you to make changes if they are needed

■ too much planning information can mean the plan is confusing or too complicated to follow easily

Planning is an important process:

■ too little planning means you may not have full control of the project

■ too much planning may result in a loss of flexibility (having to keep to a complex plan) and loss of creativity (being able to change what you are doing when new information becomes available)

the need to set out your aims clearly

You have seen that 'under-planning' and 'over-planning' make problems. As we have seen in the example on the previous page, you need to have clearly defined aims to avoid problems.

Tasks should be '**SMART**' – you may have come across this term before in your studies. SMART stands for:

Specific

Measurable

Achievable

Realistic

Time bound

■ **Specific**: an aim is specific if it is clear exactly what you have to do. 'Research VAT' is not specific but 'find two examples of goods for each of the different rates of VAT' is specific as you will know exactly what to do.

■ **Measurable:** the second aim quoted above is also measurable because it states 'find two' and 'each of the different rates' which clearly identifies what information is required. If the task had been 'find out about the goods that are subject to each rate' then you do not know how many examples to find, and you may find hundreds!

■ **Achievable:** do you have the knowledge, skills, resources and support to complete the project?

■ **Realistic:** are you able to complete the project in the time available?

■ **Time Bound** means putting time limits on the task so that it has a start and an end time, which are essential to efficient planning.

If you apply the SMART criteria to each aim in your plan you will have a clearly defined project and tasks.

monitoring your project

It is not enough just to write an Action Plan. Plans must be monitored and reviewed. Checks must take place to see if the plan is working and changes made to deal with any problems.

The most important part of any plan is the implementation – putting it into practice. The plan should include review dates when you ask the following questions:

- Am I keeping to the plan's timetable?

- Will all of the tasks be completed by the overall completion date?

- Have the completed tasks successfully achieved their aims

- Will the overall aims of the project be achieved?

If the answer to any question is no, then ask:

- If not, why not?

- Does anything need to be changed?

- How will those changes affect the overall timetable and plan?

Only by monitoring, reviewing and, if necessary, changing your plan can you make sure that it will achieve the right result on time.

completing your assessment and dealing with feedback

The assessment period for the Developing Study Skills Unit is set at between six and twelve weeks. In order to complete your Action Plan and your set piece you will need to do the following:

- agree the topic with your teacher

- state what form the presentation of your set piece will take – for example whether it is written or spoken

- create and complete your Action Plan within the 6-12 week timescale required by AAT

- receive feedback from your teacher about your Action Plan and set piece (note that you can have feedback from your teacher on a maximum of three occasions during the whole set piece/Action Plan process)

- record the feedback from your teacher in your Action Plan and state what you are going to do about the suggestions and criticisms made

- describe how your work has improved because of the feedback received, including what changes you have made

- note any problems that you have encountered and will have to solve

- give a description of the problems and the way in which you solved them

- upload different versions of your Action Plan to the AAT's learning platform, showing how the plan has changed over the period of the assessment

In the next chapter you will learn in detail about the challenges that you may encounter and how you will use feedback to solve these problems and improve your work.

Chapter Summary

- Before you start working on your set piece, you must agree your set piece and method of presentation with your tutor, along with the final completion date.

- To plan your set piece in your Action Plan you will list the tasks to be done, each broken down into smaller tasks (your 'milestones'). Each task will have its own completion date.

- You need to make sure that your tasks are listed in the correct order because some tasks will need information from previously completed tasks.

- If you do not plan in enough detail then you may miss something out and it will be difficult to estimate how much time you need for each task.

- If you spend too long planning then you will waste time that should be spent actually doing the task. You might also make it difficult to change your plan if new information is discovered.

- Your overall aim and each task should be SMART (see Key Terms on next page).

- You should build in spare time to deal with problems and plan to finish early to allow you to make changes.

- You must put review dates into your Action Plan where you will examine what has been done and what is still to do. This will help to make sure that you finish the project on time.

- Your Action Plan will be assessed as part of your overall assessment for this unit.

set piece	a piece of work or project which has been agreed with your tutor and is to be presented on an agreed date.
Action Plan	a 'to do' list of tasks with actions and resources required for each task. Expected and actual completion dates for each task are listed along with notes of any problems encountered.
target date	the date by which a task or project should be completed.
review date	the date(s) when you will check that your plan is still working and likely to allow you to finish the project on time.
under-planning	the situation where not enough detailed planning has taken place, resulting in problems.
over-planning	where the process of planning is given more importance than the completion of the tasks, resulting in problems.
SMART	this stands for:

this stands for:

Specific

Measurable

Achievable

Realistic

Time bound

the process of checking aims and tasks to see if they are SMART will ensure that the aims and tasks are clear and achievable.

Activities

7.1 Your set piece of work (choose the correct options): ✔

(a)	Can be about anything you want	
(b)	Must be agreed with your tutor	
(c)	Can be presented any way that you want	

7.2 Calum is doing a project comparing the pricing of online and 'high street' shoe shops for his set piece. He has to complete the project before 31 March. Calum has arranged an interview with the manager of a local shoe shop on the 12th March and does not want to start the project until after the interview. Calum's tutor has told him that the interview will be a good idea but there is other research that Calum can do and write up before the interview.

Tick the options that would be very useful for Calum's project: ✔

(a)	Comparing prices for 4 different brands of shoe online and in-store	
(b)	Making a list of all the shoes stocked by the shoe shop and their prices	
(c)	Writing notes on three online shoe suppliers and three 'high street' shops	

7.3 An Action Plan is (choose the most appropriate answer): ✔

(a)	An ordered list of tasks that will help you to achieve your goal	
(b)	Something to keep you busy	
(c)	A waste of time – you could just get on with the project	
(d)	A list of things to do, but in no particular order	

7.4 Sonia is trying to sort her tasks into order. She is writing a report about the theme park that was recently visited by her class. On the visit the students were given a talk about the business aspects of running a theme park and its future plans.

Sonia took some notes during the talk which she will use and took some photographs of the park but she still needs more information.

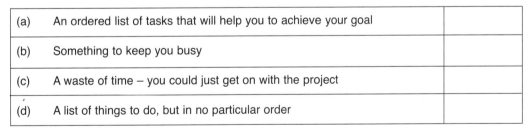

Sonia thinks that she needs to do all of the following, but she is not sure where she should start.

· Write about the visit and what she thinks about the park

· Do a cover page for the report

· Put photographs in the report to illustrate it and make it interesting

· Write about the theme park's background

· Crop photographs to use in the report

· Write about what the theme park is going to change in the future

· Find out more about the theme park's background

· Write a conclusion for the report

Decide on an appropriate order for the completion of Sonia's tasks in her Action Plan.
Write out the tasks in the order which you think is correct and number them from 1 to 8.

7.5 Your Action Plan, based on the AAT model, will need (tick all the correct answers):

(a)	A column for dates	
(b)	A column for notes	
(c)	Two columns for dates	
(d)	A task column	
(e)	An action column	
(f)	Three columns for dates	
(g)	A resources column	

7.6 Vandita has entered her tasks into her Action Plan and has allocated the same amount of time to each task. Her first tasks do not take too long so she has plenty of spare time to relax. As Vandita gets further into her project she starts to struggle to get the tasks done in time and starts to fall behind in her work.

Describe in bullet list form what Vandita could have done to avoid or sort out the problem.

(a) When she was planning her tasks.

(b) When she found that she had plenty of spare time.

(c) When she started to struggle and fall behind.

7.7   Over-planning causes the following problem (choose one):   ✔

(a)	None – you can never over plan a project	
(b)	It uses up too much paper	
(c)	It uses up too much time	

7.8   Precious likes to have everything really organised. Her tutor has given the group eight weeks to complete the set piece so Precious spends her first two weeks working on her Action Plan. Precious's tutor asks to see her Action Plan as the tutor has already seen everyone else's. Precious shows the plan to her tutor who praises the plan and gives Precious a couple of suggestions for changes. Precious spends another week working on her Action Plan to get it just right.

Although Precious's plan is very detailed, she does not complete it on time. Why do you think this is? Can you think of three reasons?

7.9   Under-planning causes the following problem (choose one):   ✔

(a)	It's not a problem as planning is a waste of time	
(b)	Important tasks may be missed or not done properly	
(c)	It makes the tutor tell you off	

7.10   Aims must be carefully thought out and written down because (choose the correct options): ✔

(a)	If they are not detailed enough then something will get missed	
(b)	If they are not clear enough then you may not know how much work to do or how many examples to find	
(c)	It will save you having to draw up a Learning Journal and an Action Plan	
(d)	It is important that they have 'to do by' dates so that all the tasks are completed by the project end date	

7.11   In order to make sure that your project is completed on time you should (choose one):   ✔

(a)	Keep working through your Action Plan without making any changes at all	
(b)	Give up using your Action Plan and carry on with the work as fast as possible	
(c)	Create review dates where you look at and, if necessary, change your Action Plan	

8 Solving problems and using feedback

this chapter covers...

This chapter builds upon the last chapter which described the writing of the Action Plan. It will help you to understand and resolve the problems that you may meet during the planning, creation and presentation of your set piece and explains:

■ *why you may not have enough information or cannot understand your information*

■ *what you have to do to make sure that you have enough information and can understand it*

■ *what causes calculation and factual errors*

■ *how to prevent an Action Plan from running late*

■ *how to prevent errors in planning*

■ *the common features of good planning and of poor planning*

■ *that problems can be prevented by good planning*

■ *how changing your plans can help you deal with common problems*

■ *that changing your plans must be recorded in your Action Plan*

The chapter also covers the importance of receiving feedback:

■ *feedback is there to help you to improve your work*

■ *feedback is about your work and not about you*

TYPES OF PROBLEM

In this chapter you will be looking at the challenges you may meet when doing your project. Whenever you work on your set piece of work and write your Action Plan you may encounter problems such as:

- lack of information
- lack of understanding
- calculation errors
- factual errors
- lack of time

These problems can be caused by one or both of the following:

- not planning your set piece of work thoroughly before you begin
- not keeping to the plans or schedules you have made

When you think you may be about to have a problem it is important to identify exactly what the problem is. Then you should take steps to stop the problem from happening if you can.

If you cannot prevent a problem occurring you then need to find out how you can solve that problem. So what causes problems and how do you prevent or solve them?

LACK OF INFORMATION AND UNDERSTANDING

Not having enough information or not understanding the information that you have can be a major problem. You cannot complete tasks properly if this is the case.

lack of information

Lack of information is where you have gaps in your instructions or gaps in your knowledge. Lack of information can be a result of:

- not keeping good records of lectures, conversations and instructions
- not learning facts and knowledge as part of your studies
- not being able to find information that you are expected to research

To prevent this lack of information you:

- need to keep good clear notes which are filed in an easy-to-find way
- should make sure that you learn the knowledge parts of the qualification

- must clearly write down instructions and check that you have got them recorded correctly

- need to be able to research information through a range of sources – as you learned in Chapter 5

lack of understanding

Lack of understanding is where you have the information but you do not understand what it means or what you have to do with the information. This can be a result of:

- not keeping good records of lectures/conversations/instructions

- not receiving clear explanations (written or verbal)

- not having enough basic knowledge about the topic or skill to allow you to understand new information or instructions

To prevent lack of understanding you:

- need to keep good clear notes which are filed so that they are easy to find

- should make sure that you learn the knowledge parts of the qualification

- must write down instructions clearly and accurately and check that you have got them recorded correctly

- must ask questions when you are given instructions or information until you are sure that you understand

DEALING WITH ERRORS

calculation errors

Calculation errors can happen and can then cause major problems. Your tutor is likely to teach you how to avoid calculation errors by:

- doing each calculation at least twice until you get the same answer twice – do not rely on your calculator the first time round!

- making sure that you write down the correct number by checking it against the calculator

- doing a calculation using two methods as a 'double check' wherever there are two ways of arriving at an answer, eg using cross casting

Cross casting is best explained using an example – see the example of cross casting in the Day Book on the next page. The word 'cast' means 'add up'.

Example:

Checking a calculation by cross casting a Sales Day Book

In a Sales Day Book (one of the books of prime entry) you should:

1   Add together the totals of the **Sales** and **VAT** columns (the figures along the bottom).

2   Add together the three totals in the **Total** column (the figures on the right-hand side).

The two figures you produce should be the same. That figure, and your 'cross casting' calculations, must therefore be correct. If they are not you must check your calculations and, if necessary, all the figures in the Sales Day Book.

Sales Day Book

Details	Invoice No	Sales £	VAT £	Total £
Salmon Ltd	Tyn00278	360.00	72.00	432.00
Pike Rivers Plc	Tyn00279	253.90	50.78	304.68
Trout & Son	Tyn00280	195.30	39.06	234.36
		809.20	161.84	971.04

Add these together to check that they equal the total of the 'Total' column:

£432.00 + £304.68 + £234.36 = **£971.04**

Add these together to check that they equal the total of the 'Total' column:
£809.20 + £161.84 = **£971.04**

factual errors

Factual errors are also a cause of problems and wrong conclusions. Either you may misread something, or the source itself may be wrong. It is therefore very important to use facts from valid and reliable sources. The internet can sometimes provide unreliable information: Wikipedia, for example, contains a great deal of useful and accurate information, but as anyone can post entries to it or edit them, some information may be incorrect.

In order to avoid factual errors you should:

- check the reliability and validity of every source that you use

- research information from more than one source: facts from different sources are seen to be reliable if they agree, along the same principle as 'cross casting' used in calculations (as above); see also the principle of 'triangulation' explained on page 70

- when you write down information that you have researched, check to make sure that you have written it down correctly

correcting errors

If you have made calculation or factual errors, you are likely to find out because your work does not make sense, facts do not match up and figures do not balance. Correcting these types of errors may require you to:

- re-calculate figures and find the correct facts

- replace the figures or facts with the correct ones

- go through your piece of work very carefully after you have found the error and change anything else that might need to be changed

the effect of errors on your Action Plan

If your piece of work relies on specific **calculations** or **facts** then finding out that some are incorrect may mean that you will need to redo some or all of your work. This will affect your schedule and plan. It is important that you are careful to check facts and calculations to prevent this from happening.

problems with wrong figures

You may sometimes make mistakes with calculations and not check them properly. If you make a mistake with a percentage calculation at the start of a piece of work, this might cause illustrations like graphs to be wrong and could lead you to make incorrect conclusions in your presentation:

example – a slip with the decimal place

You are researching a business and you calculate that 55% of its sales are online when in fact the correct figure is 5.5% of sales. You have got the decimal point in the wrong place and then assume that online sales are much more important to the business than they actually are, an incorrect conclusion.

problems with wrong facts

If you get some facts wrong your research will then be partly inaccurate, which will cost you marks in an assessment, as in the example below:

example – the wrong tax data

You are preparing a piece of work on the different rates of Income Tax and National Insurance and have gathered your information from a search on the internet. Unfortunately the source you use is old and does not quote the relevant tax year. Your data actually applies to the year 2012 and is out-of-date. Your data and findings are incorrect and you will need to do the work again.

PROBLEMS WITH TIME

In Chapter 1 you learned about looking after your time and how to draw up a work timetable. The keys to good time management are:

■ planning your time

■ using short periods of time to get short tasks done and allowing more time for longer tasks

■ doing the tasks that you need to do instead of choosing to spend a lot of time on the tasks that you know you will enjoy

running out of time – avoiding the problem

No matter how good you are at managing your time, there will be situations where you run out of time. There are a number of ways of avoiding this problem and if it does occur, putting things right:

■ having an Action Plan in place with target times and expected completion dates for each task

■ leaving room in your Action Plan in case tasks take longer than you thought they would

■ set out your Action Plan so that the final finishing date is earlier than the final date you have been given

■ regularly review the Action Plan to look for possible problems with timing

■ ask for help if you get really stuck

running out of time – steps to take

If you are working on a project and find that you are short of time then you can take the following steps:

■ review the remaining tasks and decide if they all need to be done – you may then be able to leave out some less important tasks

■ review the remaining tasks and identify which ones can be reduced in scope to take up less time

■ review the amount of time that you have allocated to each task and see if you can reduce the time to be taken in completing any of them

if you are completely stuck

If you still do not think that you can get the project and set piece completed on time, you should:

- decide how much extra time that you will need

- tell your tutor that you are having problems and ask for help and suggestions and extra time if that is possible

- make sure that you will definitely be able to finish by the new completion date if your tutor gives you extra time

Running behind time is something that can happen in any project. If you agree an extension to your deadline with your tutor you must stick to that new deadline so make sure that it is one that you can meet. You will gain respect from your tutor by meeting deadlines and communicating well.

GOOD AND POOR PLANNING

good planning

The features of effective planning and efficient organisation are:

- organising your time – this is key to success

- effective note taking and having good, simple to use, filing systems so that you can access your information (paper or electronic)

- organising your project tasks, putting them in the correct order and making sure that you know what needs to be done for each task so that you complete the project and set piece to the right standard and on time

poor planning and organisational errors

Sometimes students find that they have problems with their project because of poor planning and a lack of organisational skills. These problems are known as **organisational errors** and could happen in the following situations:

- communication – you have not communicated properly with others

- you might not have understood or remembered what other people have communicated to you – perhaps you did not note down what they said

- you may not have listed your tasks in the right order

- you may not have allocated enough time to each task

- you may have missed tasks out

- you may not have clearly identified what you need to do for each task

If this happens you should take the following steps:

- identify what has gone wrong

- identify what you should do to avoid the error in future projects
- decide what needs to be done now to correct the error
- rewrite your Action Plan – you should make sure that your new plan includes all changes needed to all tasks and that any changes in schedule will allow you to finish on time

It is important for your skills development and for your future work that you do not just fix the problem now but that you understand what has gone wrong and how to prevent the problem in the future. You do not want to keep making the same planning mistakes again and again.

The example that follows shows how and why a project can go wrong and the steps that can be taken to put things right with the project and its plan.

Example: Ava's project

Ava is planning to write a report about accounting firms in the area. Ava has decided to try to find out how many there are within 20 miles of her home. She intends to find out what sort of work that they do and what qualifications they ask their staff to have.

Ava writes her Action Plan, agrees it with her teacher and starts working on the plan.

- One week into her plan, Ava has researched and found a number of firms.
- Ava spends another week deciding what information she needs and putting together a list of questions.
- Ava chooses 10 firms and sends them emails explaining what she is doing and asking them to answer some questions.

A week later none of them has replied. A couple of days later, Ava, who is upset, goes to her teacher for advice.

After talking to her teacher, she sends another 10 emails to firms, using her college email address rather than her own 'AmazingPrincessAva@yahoo.com' email address. Ava also checks the text of her email with her teacher who advises her about the way she needs to word the message, laying it out formally and using business language.

This time she gets two replies by the end of the day and over the next week Ava gets four more replies that were very helpful. Following the teacher's advice, Ava and her study buddy go to a meeting of their local AAT member's branch with some questionnaires. The branch members were really helpful and also talked about working in industry as well as in practice.

Ava finally has the information that she needs but it has taken five weeks instead of three. Ava has only got one week left before her report is due.

What went wrong?

Ava had communication problems with the firms because:

- Ava's original email was not properly worded and had an unprofessional email address; this made the accounting firms concerned about the student who was contacting them.
- Ava's unusual personal email may therefore have gone into the firm's junk email folder.

- Ava's Action Plan underestimated how long it would take to get the information and did not include the visit to the local AAT branch.

In future, when communicating with businesses, Ava needs to communicate using formal business communication methods. Ava also needs to plan to use a range of methods for getting information and not assume that one method (emailing the firms and asking them) will be enough.

Amending Ava's Action Plan

Ava now has one week left before her deadline. Ava reviewed her Action Plan and . . .

- took out anything that was not absolutely necessary, for example finding a picture for the cover page
- focused first on sorting out the information from the firms
- then focused on writing the report

Ava then looked at how much time she had available and how much time that she thought she needed to complete her new Action Plan.

Ava went back to her teacher and asked for an extra week. The teacher agreed because Ava had kept her teacher informed all along about the problems she had encountered.

a successful result

Ava handed in her report to her teacher by the new deadline date.

the need to recognise mistakes

The lesson to be learnt from the above example is that Ava needed to recognise problems as they happened and also the mistakes she had made. She would then be able to tackle problems as they arose with the help and advice of her teacher.

Ava's main problem was her lack of sufficient planning and a major issue was the use of an unprofessional email address. Her strength lay in her readiness to act on the advice of her teacher and to then be able to hand in her report by the revised deadline. This is all part of the learning process.

THE NEED FOR FEEDBACK

what is feedback?

Feedback is very simply a comment made about the work that you have done

Feedback can be both **negative** and **positive**:

■ **negative feedback** is a criticism of where you have gone wrong in your work which then puts you off doing that work

■ **positive feedback** involves comments on what you have already done which makes you want to change and improve on what you have done

People react better to positive feedback than to negative feedback. Positive feedback is motivational and negative feedback can have the opposite effect, although a 'wake-up call' can make people take action to solve a problem.

Feedback is not something that you will only get once, it happens at several times at intervals in your course and aims to improve your performance. This regular feedback is called **formative feedback** – it puts you on the right path and means that you will stand a better chance of success in your assessment. Formative feedback is shown below as a circular process.

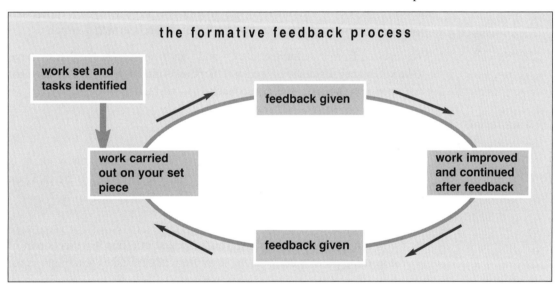

the formative feedback process

why is feedback important?

Making the most of feedback is an important part of developing your study skills:

■ it helps you to perform at your best at different stages of your course

■ it makes you aware of your strengths and identifies areas for improvement

■ it allows you to plan ahead for actions which will improve performance

Getting feedback during this AAT Unit will be important as you will need to use it when completing and refining the Learning Journal and the Action Plan. Feedback on your work can come from three main sources: your **tutor**, your **fellow students** and **you**.

We will now describe these three sources of feedback in detail.

feedback from your tutor

Your tutor will give you feedback on your work for this Unit on at least one occasion, but you will not receive more than three pieces of formal written feedback. Each time you receive this feedback you will also need to respond formally. This feedback can be:

■ during the writing of your **Action Plan**; this will require documentation of your response in your Action Plan

■ on the presentation of your **set piece of work** with tutor recommendations of how the presentation could be improved followed by your comments on how the presentation has been improved

In addition **informal** feedback (eg verbal feedback) may be made by your tutor about your **Learning Journal** – this will point out how you can improve on your work; this feedback and the way in which you respond to it should be included in the comments column in the Learning Journal.

You can see from this that feedback – and your responses to feedback – have to be taken very seriously indeed and that the results of your final assessment rest upon your attitude to that feedback.

hints on using tutor feedback

Good feedback from your tutor will help you to improve your work. It is sometimes not pleasant receiving feedback on your work if you are told you need to make lots of changes, but you should remember:

■ no-one is perfect

■ the first time you do something you may need to refine it – this is part of the learning process and you can learn from any mistakes you might make

■ even when you are experienced, you may still make errors or go in the wrong direction from time to time

■ the person giving feedback about your work is trying to help

■ feedback is not about you as a person, it is only about improving your work

So how do you use the feedback?

Feedback is about commenting on your work. When you receive the comments from your tutor you should:

■ listen or read (as appropriate) carefully and make notes if necessary

■ make sure that you understand everything

■ go away and think about it, for a day or so if you can

- decide what you agree with and what you might want to question
- ask your tutor questions to clarify any points you are not sure about

When you have thought about the feedback, you should:

- make the suggested changes to your work where you agree with the feedback (there will always be some things that you haven't thought of)
- justify/discuss any changes where you do not agree with the feedback and agree what further changes are needed
- remember that if you are discussing feedback with your tutor, then you need to be careful about not acting on your tutor's suggestions – make sure that you consider this carefully and discuss why you disagree, backing this up with some evidence
- finally – make any changes that are still needed after the discussions

After making changes and finishing your project, think about the changes made after feedback:

- what changed as a result of the feedback?
- did the feedback make the end result better? Why? How?
- what can I do better the next time I do this sort of project?

Remember that feedback is not personal and not about you – it is there to help you in your work.

methods of tutor feedback

There are a number of ways in which a tutor may provide you with feedback: written feedback forms, written comments on your work and verbal feedback in class or a tutorial session

■ formal feedback form

In a formal feedback form there is usually a list of areas for review, space for the reviewer to comment and then room for the reviewer to document any discussion, including comments from the student. This type of documentation can form part of a **structured review** process required by the teaching centre.

The form will usually have a heading and dates, together with space for longer comments and further documents to be attached.

■ informal notes from the tutor

If the tutor comments are part of a less formal feedback process they can just be listed on a piece of paper in note form, or even made verbally.

A tutor's notes and a formal feedback form are illustrated on the next page.

informal notes from the tutor

NOTES ON ACTION PLAN – ANNA ALLIEVO

1. Overall a good Action Plan with all the columns used correctly.

2. It might be helpful to break task 6 into two tasks, perhaps we could have a chat about it?

3. The second task 'find pictures' should not take long – do you think that you could finish it a bit sooner?

G. Lehrer, 3 March 20XX

formal feedback form including comments on the tutor's notes shown above

ACTION PLAN FEEDBACK DOCUMENT

Writer's Name: A Allievo   **Tutor's Name:** G Lehrer

Date of first feedback: 3/3/20XX   **Date of second feedback**: 7/3/20XX

Subject	Tutor comments	Student reply	Tutor 2nd comment
Are the entries in the 'Actions required' column complete?	Yes		
Are the tasks all appropriate in size and content?	Task 6 is large and might be better broken into two tasks.	I think it is better kept as one task for the reasons we discussed.	I accept your reasons for keeping task 6 as one task. Thank you.
Does every task have an appropriate target date?	The second task 'find pictures' has been given a lot of time, can this time be reduced?	Eight pictures must be found, but I will agree to reduce the time by half.	Thank you. I think this will give you more time to focus on important tasks such as the research. Pictures are just there to illustrate your work.

feedback from other students

You may or may not like feedback and criticism from other students, but it can be very useful. Comments and advice from fellow students can help if you do not understand a certain topic and are possibly making mistakes in your work.

Situations where you could try to get useful feedback from other students include:

- when you do group work

- if you have a study buddy (or buddies)

This type of feedback will obviously not form part of the formal feedback you will receive from your tutor, but can certainly help your learning and improve your final project.

reviewing your own work

As well as other people reviewing your work, you should review it yourself.

Here are some tips:

- check your work from time-to-time to make sure you have done everything according to plan

- re-calculate any calculations a few days after you originally did them

- use a spell check if it is available – but make sure it is UK English rather than American English!

- print out your work so that you can read it on paper rather than on the screen

- make sure that you read every word, including headings – the writer is often the last person to spot a spelling or grammatical mistake

- read your work out loud or, if you can't actually read it out loud, pretend to read it out loud in your head

family and friends

Lastly, it is often useful to get a member of your family, a friend or a close partner to read your work for you.

You should only ask this if they have enough time and you are comfortable that you may possibly get some critical comments from them. You do not want to spoil family relations or a beautiful partnership in the process!

Chapter Summary

■ Problems can be caused by poor planning and/or by a failure to carry out plans properly.

■ To prevent a lack of information or understanding you must make clear notes, learn facts and check instructions.

■ If you cannot find the information or understand what you are doing you must keep asking questions and checking your work.

■ Calculation and factual errors can be prevented by regular checking.

■ You have to manage your time by organising it and using small amounts of time to complete short tasks.

■ If you are short of time then you should review what you have planned to do, to see whether you actually need to carry out all of the tasks.

■ You can review the amount of time allocated to each task to see if you can do them more quickly.

■ If you need to ask for extra time on a project, make sure that you do this in plenty of time and complete it by the new date.

■ Good planning is achieved by organising your time, effective note taking and sorting your tasks into the right order.

■ Poor planning can result from poor communication, lack of understanding or missing things out.

■ If your planning goes wrong then you must identify what went wrong so that it does not happen again, and then correct what you have done.

■ Feedback – which can be formal or informal – will help you to identify weaknesses in your work and to improve it.

■ Feedback can be positive or negative, but you will need to be able to react positively to either type.

■ Feedback can be from your tutor, other students, family and friends.

■ Feedback can also – importantly – come from yourself: you will need to read, check and go over your set piece very carefully before finally submitting it for assessment.

Key Terms		
	factual errors	incorrect facts or information – these kinds of errors may lead to the wrong decisions being made
	triangulation	checking the accuracy of information by referring to more than one source
	calculation errors	mistakes made while calculating figures
	cross casting	adding up two sets of figures to obtain the same total – this will confirm the accuracy of the total
	organisational errors	mistakes made when organising tasks, including missing out or taking too much time over tasks
	negative feedback	a criticism of where you have gone wrong in your work which then puts you off doing that work
	positive feedback	helpful and constructive comments on what you have already done which makes you want to change and improve on what you have done
	formal feedback	part of a structured review process required by the teaching centre – this is normally given on a structured form which sets out the points made by the tutor and requires written responses from the student
	informal feedback	feedback that is not formal – examples include verbal comments or written lists of suggestions and criticisms from the tutor to the student
	formative feedback	positive feedback is given to improve performance – this type of feedback is given at regular intervals in a project such as in tutorial meetings

Activities

In questions where you have to choose one or more options, tick the correct answer(s).

Note that there may be more than one correct answer to a question.

8.1 You discover that you have an incorrect website address in your set piece references. What type of error is this? (choose one answer):

(a)	Calculation error	
(b)	Factual error	
(c)	Feedback error	

8.2 Chloe has asked her study buddy, Kamila to read her work to check that it makes sense. Kamila asks Chloe a lot of questions about a section of the work where Kamila does not really understand what she is reading. Chloe tries to answer but is not really able to explain in a way that Kamila understands. What do you think that Chloe should do next?

(a)	Re-write the part that Kamilla does not understand	
(b)	Review the topic to make sure that she fully understands it herself	

8.3 When you add up a column of figures you should: (choose one answer):

(a)	Quickly add it up on your calculator and move on to the next calculation	
(b)	Estimate approximately what the total will be and then add the column up on your calculator and use that total if it is anywhere near your estimate	
(c)	Add the column up at least twice until you get the same answer twice	

8.4 Royston is running behind with his college project which has to be completed within six weeks. He reviewed what he had done after two weeks and found that everything was on schedule, but after another two weeks he finds he is running nearly a week late.

This means that Royston has two weeks left to do three weeks' work and he is sure that he cannot complete all of the planned tasks on time.

What should Royston do now? Tick the options that would be suitable courses of action for Royston to take.

(a)	Review the remaining tasks and see which ones can be discarded	
(b)	Review the remaining tasks and see which ones can be reduced in scope	
(c)	Review the time allocated to the new list of tasks and see where the time allocated to each task could be reduced	

8.5   If you find that you have made a minor mistake in your project work, what should you do? (choose all that apply).

(a)	Sort out the problem as quickly as possible	
(b)	Hide it so that non-one notices what you have done	
(c)	Decide what you should do to try to prevent it from happening again	

8.6   If you find that you have made a major mistake in your project work, what should you do? (choose all that apply).

(a)	Look for an alternative project for the set piece	
(b)	Ask for help from your teacher	
(c)	Adapt your Action Plan to get the project back on track	

8.7   A group of students has been asked to give feedback to each other about their presentations which form part of their set piece of work. This type of feedback is (choose one answer):

(a)	Formal	
(b)	Informal	
(c)	Organisational	

8.8   Formative feedback is (choose one answer):

(a)	Positive feedback which encourages you to improve what you have already done	
(b)	Negative feedback which just points out what you have done wrong	

9 Presenting your set piece

this chapter covers...

In this chapter you will learn about the different ways of presenting your set piece, whether in writing or in front of an audience. You will be guided on how to choose an appropriate method for you and also how to present your work. This chapter will explain that:

- *the method you use to present your work – eg a report, a presentation with slides – will depend on what type of information you are presenting*

- *you can improve your writing skills with practice*

- *you should keep your writing simple, using the correct language*

- *your work should be clearly laid out to make it easy to read and understand*

- *your written and orally presented work must be presented in a logical order*

- *being a confident presenter is about being prepared and following simple rules*

- *if you give an oral presentation with slides, they should be simple and uncluttered*

- *you can combine written and orally presented work, for example a set piece in the form of a discussion requires both written work and preparation of a verbal presentation*

PRESENTING YOUR SET PIECE

the subject of the set piece

In Chapter 7 you learned that you will have to complete a set piece of work which you will present when you finish this Unit. The piece of work can:

- relate to any AAT unit you are studying

- be about your own personal development

- be a research project on an aspect of accounting or business

- be about a completely different topic, not related to the course

You also learned that you will have to agree your set piece and your presentation methods with your tutor in advance, writing up this information in your Action Plan.

the different presentation methods

This chapter describes the different methods of presentation that you can use. These include:

- a written report

- a presentation to an individual or group using presentation software

- a verbal presentation, possibly involving a discussion of a piece of work

- any combination of these methods of presentation

The purpose of the set piece of work is to help you improve these two areas:

- your subject knowledge

- your planning and presentation skills

This is why you have a wide choice of topics which you can cover.

WHAT TYPE OF PRESENTATION METHOD SHOULD YOU USE?

the planning process

Your presentation method will:

- be agreed in advance with your tutor

- be written into your action plan

- depend upon your choice of set piece and your tutor's guidance

making your choice of presentation method

The method that you use for you presentation will depend on which methods you are most comfortable with and what your strongest skills are eg:

- writing a report – how good are you at writing?
- using presentation software – how confident are you speaking to a group of people?

When making your choice of presentation method you must:

- choose a method that best suits the piece of work you are presenting
- realise that the chosen method may not be your favourite presentation method
- be able to justify your choice of presentation method, stating why you chose that method
- realise that you can mix presentation methods – writing part of your set piece and then presenting it orally or discussing it

other factors affecting your choice

The table below shows other things that you should consider when making your choice of presentation method. It will help to guide you to select the method that suits you best.

presentation method	when this method will be most effective and useful
written presentation: text, tables, diagrams	• You need to present a lot of detailed information, eg visual information such as graphs and diagrams. • The people receiving the information may need to refer back to it later on for guidance. • The people receiving the information may be in different locations.
oral presentation using presentation software	• You need to inform a group of people all at once. • You want to introduce or give a summary of a complex subject. • You want to start a discussion to produce new ideas. • You want to help people to make a decision. • You want to put your views across and get support from others. • You are expecting a lot of questions.
verbal discussion – with text and diagrams	• You need to introduce complex information and then get other people's opinions about it. • You are presenting to a small group of people. • You want to discuss new ideas. • You need to persuade people to accept your opinions or ideas.

PRESENTING YOUR WORK IN WRITTEN FORM

advantages

The advantage of presenting work in writing is that:

- you can present to many people in many different locations
- your readers can refer back to the written work at any time to revise what they have learned
- you can provide detailed information that the reader can take in and understand at a time and place that suits them

keeping it simple and clear

The most important thing about presenting any work is that it is **clear** and **easy to understand**. This means that it must:

- use simple language that the reader will understand
- be clearly laid out to make it easy to find information
- be in a logical order that makes sense

writing tips

Although a lot of people worry about producing formal pieces of writing, like all skills, you can improve your writing standard and style with practice.

When you are writing a report it is important that you use formal language – but note that this is a little different from everyday speech:

- use simple words that you are sure that you understand
- use the right words to make sure that you are understood – but do not try to impress by using long words if you are not sure what they mean
- shorter, clearer sentences are better than long complicated ones
- don't use 'slang' or the informal language you use when chatting with friends – eg if you write 'the new high speed train was really cool' a reader might think that the air conditioning had been turned up too high
- do not use words such as 'don't' and 'shouldn't' – this is how you would say them, but in formal writing you should use 'do not' and 'should not'
- if you want to use initials to shorten a name like 'Association of Accounting Technicians', write the words out full the first time with the abbreviation after it in brackets; once you have quoted the initials 'AAT', you can then use them in the text that follows
- break your writing up by using headings and short paragraphs
- start a new paragraph every time you start a new topic

- try to begin the new paragraph with a linking sentence to guide your reader by introducing the new topic, for example: 'The next area to be covered is active and passive learning'

- if you find you are repeating the same word a lot, a useful way of finding an alternative word with the same meaning (a '**synonym**') is to look in a **thesaurus** (a kind of dictionary that gives you other words with the same meaning rather than the meaning of the word you are looking up). You can find a thesaurus online if you do a Web search on 'thesaurus' – all modern word processing software (eg Word) have a built in thesaurus

- use a clear, professional font that is easy to read for your work and for all other business documents; good examples of professional fonts are:

  Arial   Helvetica   Calibri   Times

- avoid fancy fonts which can be distracting and difficult to read, eg:

  Vivaldi   **Comic Sans**   *Zapf Chancery*   Oxford

- use a font size that is easy to read, for example: 10 point or 11 point

- use larger font sizes or **bold type** to make your main headings and subheadings stand out from the body of the text

- remember to number your pages and provide an index if required

making your written work look good

Presenting your work in a neat and tidy way which is clear and easy to read is important as this will make a good impression on your reader. It is important that your work has a logical order; a formal written piece of work will usually have the following sections:

- a cover page

- an introduction which tells the reader what the work is going to include and what the reader will learn

- the main part of the work

- a conclusion which tells the reader what has been learned

The main part of the work may be broken into sections which cover different topics, in the same way that chapters in this book have sections within them.

Your assessor will get a positive 'first impression' of your written work if:

- you have taken time and care over the presentation and content

- your work is laid out clearly and is easy to read so that the assessor can easily find and take in the information presented

If your work is untidy then your assessor will:

- think that you do not really care about your work

- find it difficult to read the work

- find it difficult to find specific information within your work

format for a simple report

Set out below is an example of how you should lay out a simple written report, a useful format for presenting a written set piece.

Title Page

Title

Student name

Date

Introduction

The introduction will tell the reader what is coming in the main section.

It need not be long and it normally includes why you are doing the report.

Main Section

The main section can have headings for different topics.

Space the work out. If there is not much room at the end of a page, start a new topic on a new page.

Conclusion

This tells the reader what has been said in the report and what conclusions have been reached.

It may also contain recommendations for further action.

organising your main section in a logical order

Your main body/findings section will need to be presented in a logical order. The information should flow from the beginning to the end in a clear way which is easy for the reader to follow. This is shown in the diagram below.

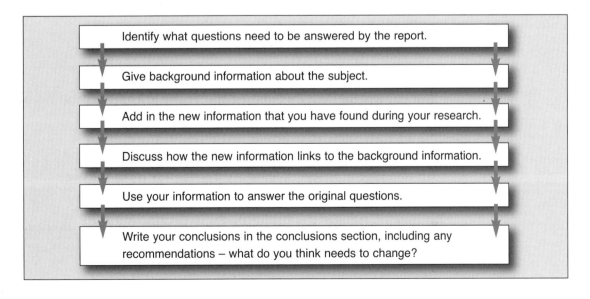

Identify what questions need to be answered by the report.

Give background information about the subject.

Add in the new information that you have found during your research.

Discuss how the new information links to the background information.

Use your information to answer the original questions.

Write your conclusions in the conclusions section, including any recommendations – what do you think needs to change?

a note on formal reports

You will come across elsewhere in your studies ('Working in Accounting and Finance') a **formal report** format which contains extra sections such as appendices and recommendations, but you do not need to worry about these for the Study Skills Unit. The simple report format shown on the previous page provides a very useful structure for a written set piece.

using the computer for writing your set piece

When you are writing on a computer, you do not necessarily have to write the content in the final order of presentation. You can:

- enter a series of topic headings to make sure that you are covering everything

- decide on a logical order for these sections

- start by filling in the sections that you are comfortable with, and already have the information for, to give you confidence – then work through the rest of the document, making sure that you complete every section

- identify your spelling mistakes in the text – using a spellcheck set to UK English – and make the corrections

- print the document if possible and then read it carefully

- double check any calculations

- check the layout carefully, including headings, bullets and tables

- ask your study buddy or someone else to review your work and give you feedback and make any agreed changes that are needed

- read your work again for another (hopefully final) check

USING PRESENTATION SOFTWARE

Your set piece may take the form of a presentation to a large or small group using presentation software such as PowerPoint.

advantages

The advantage of presenting information in this way is that you can:

- inform a group of people all at once

- start a discussion and ask your listeners to think about the subject in different ways

- answer questions immediately

format of a presentation

Your presentation should normally be given in the following order:

- an introduction – where you tell your audience why you are presenting on this topic and give an outline of what is to be discussed
- the main section – this will be broken down into topics
- a summary – where you summarise the main points of the presentation
- a conclusion – where you can make recommendations for action

You will need to produce the visual presentation well in advance, practise it and make sure that you have the right equipment available in the room where you are to make your presentation.

tips for using presentation software

The basic rules of using presentation software are:

- keep it simple
- keep the slides tidy, free from clutter
- a little information on each slide is much better than too much
- make sure that your slides can be seen and read from the back of the room

animation and colour

Many students spend a lot of time choosing templates and colours, putting lots of pictures on slides and having exciting animation where words and pictures are flying everywhere across the screen. Good presenters are more interested in getting their facts across than showing how 'whizzy' they are with the software. Here are some guidelines for dealing with animation and colour if you are planning to use them:

- discuss and agree with your tutor **what type** and **how much** animation is needed for assessment purposes – and decide if it is necessary

- write the content of the slides first, adding any necessary pictures

- decide what you are going to say in your presentation about each slide

- only when you have written the slides should you choose the slide themes and colours to make them look good – remembering to make sure that any writing and pictures are clearly visible

- only animate after you know what you are going to say so that you have the right words appearing on the screen in the right order for you to provide your spoken commentary

Study the examples of slides on the next page – they show the different types of information that can be used in a visual presentation and help to explain the 'do's' and 'don'ts' of using slides.

Example: suggested formats for different types of slide

first slide, showing the title of your set piece

Header Slide

Title of your Set Piece

text slides – any number (within reason) can be used

Text slides

- You can use bullet points to list information
- Keep the font size big
- Keep the points short
- Use simple language
- Remember that the presenter will be providing an oral explanation of the content
- Do not use too much information on each slide

using text and relevant pictures on one slide – the two should ideally not overlap as pictures can distract from the text and even make it unreadable, as in the case of the fifth bullet point here

Text and picture slides

- Use varied layouts for your slides.
- Combine text and pictures in different ways.
- Take care to make sure the meaning is clear
- Do not let the picture dominate the design.
- Avoid writing over pictures, you may not always be able to read the text!
- Avoid writing over pictures, you may not always be able to read the text!

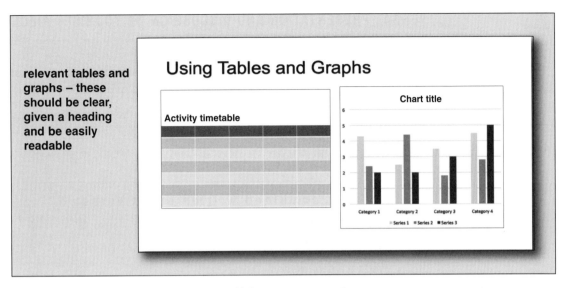

relevant tables and graphs – these should be clear, given a heading and be easily readable

being a confident presenter

Being a confident presenter is about being prepared. Plan your presentation in advance and rehearse it until you are comfortable with the content. Most experienced presenters always practise their presentations at least once and usually several times before the actual presentation.

Here are some tips on presenting:

- make sure that you know your subject really well

- practice until you are confident

- have notes to remind you what you want to say in case you forget – notes on index cards or on printouts of the slides can be very useful

- speak up and speak clearly, not too quickly or too slowly, and give plenty of eye contact – do not bury your head in your notes

- make sure you have timed your presentation during your rehearsal to check it is the right length for the time you are allowed

- plan extra things to talk about if you finish early or be prepared to miss out less important slides if you run late

- think about the sort of questions that may be asked and prepare for them

- a confident and well-groomed personal appearance will make things go better – prepare yourself well, avoid a late night out on the previous evening and have something to eat and drink before you give your presentation

Remember:
A common mistake made by a lot of inexperienced presenters is that they prepare slides with long sentences that look like a speech and then read out every word. This will have the audience asleep in no time.

VERBAL PRESENTATION AND DISCUSSION OF YOUR SET PIECE

You may present your work to your tutor as part of a meeting. This way of presenting work is a combination of a written and oral presentation format.

In this case you will hand over a document similar to the written reports and then will then discuss the content.

The process looks like this:

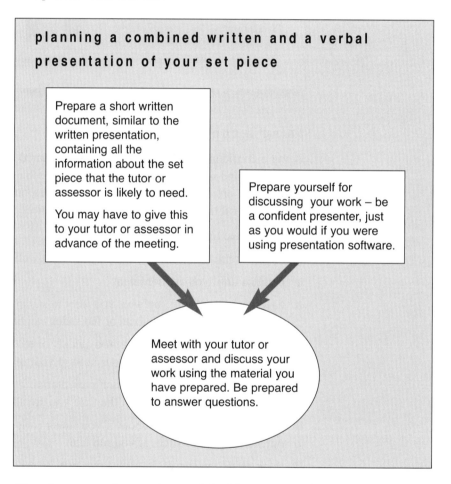

planning a combined written and a verbal presentation of your set piece

Prepare a short written document, similar to the written presentation, containing all the information about the set piece that the tutor or assessor is likely to need.

You may have to give this to your tutor or assessor in advance of the meeting.

Prepare yourself for discussing your work – be a confident presenter, just as you would if you were using presentation software.

Meet with your tutor or assessor and discuss your work using the material you have prepared. Be prepared to answer questions.

The advantages of presenting work in this way are as follows:

■ you can explain aspects of written reports in more detail, immediately answering questions that the tutor may have

■ you will avoid having to stand up to give a presentation to a group of people, a process which makes some people very nervous

Chapter Summary

- Written reports are useful when you need to provide information to a large number of people.

- Written reports are appropriate for detailed work or work that will need to be referred back to over time.

- Writing is a skill that you can learn and improve.

- There are a number of guidelines that can help your writing skills, like keeping your sentences short.

- Making your writing look good by laying it out clearly will make it easier to read and understand.

- Arranging your work in a logical order is important.

- You do not necessarily need to write the work in the same order as you present the work – you should start where you feel most confident.

- Check your work thoroughly and get a study buddy to do another check if you can.

- Presenting using presentation software is a good way of informing a group of people at the same time.

- Giving a presentation allows you to start a discussion and share ideas.

- Presenting to a group is useful if you want to persuade the audience to agree with your opinion on an issue.

- A verbal discussion about written work allows questions to be dealt with quickly.

- When using presentation software, keep the slides simple and easy to read.

- Do not over animate your slides – this will distract attention from the content.

- Practising and thinking of the type of questions that will be asked will help you to present confidently.

- Do not read out the slides!

- Before a verbal presentation to your tutor, you will need to produce written work and also prepare for a discussion (as you would a presentation to a group).

synonym	a word that has the same or similar meaning to another word – a substitute word that can be used to replace a word that you do not want to use or to use too many times
thesaurus	a form of dictionary (also available online) that gives a range of alternative words which have the same meaning as the word you are looking up
introduction	the first part of a report/set piece where you write or tell the reader (or audience) what your presentation will contain, why the piece of work has been set and the purpose of the work
main section	the main body of your report/set piece where you set out all the relevant information – it is usually broken down into sections with headings
summary	this section briefly repeats the main points of your work
conclusion	this summarises the findings and may contain recommendations for further action
formal report	a more extended report structure containing separate sections of recommendations and appendices (reference material) note: *a formal report will not be required for this Unit, although knowledge of its contents may be examined in the 'Working in Accounting and Finance' Unit*
animation	elements on presentation slides which can be made to move, for example words appearing and objects flying around on the screen
template	a set layout that can be used to set out individual slides of a presentation

Activities

In questions where you have to choose one or more options, tick the correct answer(s).

Note that there may be more than one correct answer to a question.

9.1 As part of his project work Sanjay has carried out a survey of his fellow students' views on drinking and driving. He has circulated a questionnaire about this and has then issued some written details of its findings to his class. This shows that opinions are very divided. How should he take his project forward so that he can reach some final conclusions? (choose one answer):

✔

(a)	Produce a written report	
(b)	Make an oral presentation to a group with presentation software	
(c)	Arrange a verbal discussion of the issues raised by the questionnaire	

9.2 Phoebe has also chosen the topic of diet for her set piece. She is hoping to educate her classmates about diet and persuade them that a healthy low fat diet is essential for long-term health. Which presentation method should she use? (choose one answer):

✔

(a)	Written notes with diagrams	
(b)	Presentation to her class illustrated by projected slides	
(c)	Formal written report	

9.3 Polly is writing a report on Sustainability as her set piece. She has written the following paragraph:

> *'Sustainability is about managing the natural environment for the future which includes making sure that global warming doesn't happen so bad and sustainability is also about making sure that there is economic growth with businesses that work and it's also about making sure that everyone in society is looked after and treated, like, fairly.'*

(a) Examine the words that Polly has used in this paragraph. Some of Polly's writing is not in business language.

Identify **three words or phrases** that are not appropriate for inclusion in a written report.

(b) Polly has used one long sentence for the whole paragraph.

Re-word the paragraph into **three sentences**, improving the text by replacing and/or moving any words or phrases that you think need changing.

9.4 The main benefits of a clearly laid out report are (choose one): ✔

(a)	It is easier for the reader to find information	
(b)	There are no benefits; the information is all there, you just have to read it	
(c)	It shows that you are a very well organised person	

9.5 Sort the following headings into the correct order for a presentation:

(a) Recommendations

(b) Linking new information to background information

(c) Background information

(d) Conclusions

(e) Purpose of the report

(f) Questions to be answered

(g) New information

9.6 Before presenting your written work, you should (choose one): ✔

(a)	Finish writing and hand it in straightaway	
(b)	Ask your Study Buddy to read it through and make any necessary changes	
(c)	Email it and assume you will not have to read it	

9.7 Shiva has animated his slides so that each sentence and picture spins or bounces onto the screen. What feedback might Shiva get on his slides from his tutor? (Choose all that apply). ✔

(a)	The animation was distracting	
(b)	The animation was appropriate	
(c)	The animation caused the talk to go slowly	

Environmental Pollution

- There is an urgent need for businesses and individuals to become 'green' and adopt policies which protect the environment, save energy and benefit society as a whole.

- The need to protect the environment and conserve resources – the 'green' factor – is one that is most commonly associated with sustainability.

- Examples of 'green' policies which can be adopted by businesses include 'cycle to work' schemes and car sharing, initiatives in the workplace to reduce the consumption of electricity, for example 'turn off the lights and the computers at night' campaigns together with energy-saving devices such as LED and low-energy lights.

- Materials should be manufactured from from sustainable resources (for example books printed on paper manufactured from forests which are being replanted rather than being depleted) and also recycling of waste materials such as paper, plastic, cardboard

9.8   Brad is worried about his presentation slide (shown above) which deals with sustainability. He does not like the design and thinks the slide is cluttered. Identify three main design mistakes that Brad has made.

9.9   Luis is planning his speech to go with his set piece slides. What are the main things he should think about to make the best impression in his class presentation? (choose all that apply)   ✔

(a)	What he is going to say	
(b)	What he is going to wear	
(c)	Having extra topics to talk about if he finishes earlier than expected	
(d)	What questions might be asked	
(e)	How many times he should do a practice run through	
(f)	How to make sure he does not leave anything out	

9.10   Naomi does not like presenting to a group so is going to present her work to her tutor at a meeting with him. In order to prepare for this Naomi should think about (choose all that apply):   ✔

(a)	What she is going to say	
(b)	How her written work will be laid out	
(c)	Extra topics to talk about if she finishes earlier than expected	
(d)	What questions might be asked	
(e)	How many times she should do a practice run through	
(f)	How she can make a good impression on the tutor	

Answers to activities

CHAPTER 1: INTRODUCTION TO STUDY SKILLS

1.1   (a)   The journal itself will be assessed

(b)   You will have to answer questions about what you have learned by keeping your Learning Journal during your studies

(c)   You need to be able to talk about entries in your Learning Journal in your assessment

1.2   (b)   2

1.3   (a)   2 minutes

1.4   (c)   A topic that you find hard and don't get correct

1.5   (a)   Yes, it helps the brain organise and sort information

1.6   (b)   False

1.7   (a)   It makes learning more interesting

(b)   It helps you to put information in your long-term memory

1.8   (a)   True

CHAPTER 2: CREATING THE LEARNING JOURNAL

2.1   (a)   It will help you progress in your career if you are good at learning

(c)   It makes it easier for you to learn, and will enable you to enjoy your learning

(d)   The more you learn properly, the more you will be able to learn

2.2   (b)   A record of your learning activities

(c)   A way of learning about what methods of learning suit you

(d)   A way of learning how to improve your learning methods

2.3   (a)   Making entries after every study session

(c)   Completing the journal accurately

(d)   Recording your thoughts honestly

2.4   (c)   Learning Activity

(d)   Learning Style

2.5   (b)   'I had difficulty with double-entry: I understand that I need to debit the bank to put money in and credit the bank to take money out, but I don't really understand the difference between expenses and liabilities.'

2.6   (a)   Identify which learning styles work well and which are poor learning styles for you

(b)   Record experiments in which you use different learning methods

2.7   (c)   I will need to write about things that are recorded in my journal, identifying entries in my journal as evidence

CHAPTER 3: LEARNING STYLES

3.1   (b)   Visual Auditory Kinesthetic

3.2   (d)   Interactive e-learning

3.3   (a)   True

3.4   (i)   (b)   Auditory
         (ii)   (a)   Visual

3.5   (c)   Kinesthetic

3.6   (a)   Short-term memory

3.7   (a)   Facts
         (c)   Simple routine calculations

3.8   (a)   Questioning
         (b)   Choosing key words to note
         (d)   Linking to concepts that are already understood

3.9   (a)   True

3.10 (b)   Long-term memory

3.11 (a)   Keep trying the calculation in different ways until he gets the correct answer
         (b)   Talk about it with Rose, his Study Buddy
         (c)   Try to explain the calculation to a non-accounting friend
         (d)   Have a go, get an answer and compare it with Rose's answer

3.12 (a)   True

CHAPTER 4: LEARNING ACTIVITIES

4.1

Learning Activity	VAK?	Active or Passive?
Watching a video presentation or film	VA	P
Practising the same calculation (with different numbers) over and over again	VK	P
Practice questions that need thinking about	VK	A
Reading	V	P
Teacher talking or lecturing	VA	P
Working on a problem in pairs	VAK	A
Research on a computer	VK	A
Look at a given computer website	V	P
Demonstration – you are shown how to do something	VA	P
You explain or demonstrate to another person	VAK	A
Research using books and journals	V	A
Group discussion	VAK	A
Pair discussion	VAK	A
Scenario or case studies done individually	VK	A
Scenario or case studies done in pairs	VAK	A
Scenario or case studies done in groups	VAK	A
Multiple choice quiz	VK	A
Puzzles	VK	A
Checking other student's work	VK	A
You give a presentation to the class on your own	VAK	A
You are part of a group presenting information to the class	VAK	A
Preparing researched information to present to the class	VAK	A

4.2   (b)   The group work may be delayed or not as good as it could have been

         (c)   Chelsea learns less than she would have learned if she had engaged

4.3   (a)   Learning actively

4.4   (a)   What to say

         (b)   How to explain what you are going to say

4.5   Possible ways:

- Making notes and thinking about what is being read.
- Asking yourself questions and linking what you are reading to what you already know about the topic.

4.6   (a)   Hugh and his friends are making the learning more visual, auditory and kinesthetic.

         (b)   They are also increasing the active part of the learning.

4.7   (a)   You feel supported

         (b)   You have someone to study with

4.8   (a)   True

4.9   (a)   True

4.10 (a)   At home

         (b)   At college

         (d)   At any time that is convenient to Patrick

4.11 (a)   They make her think

         (b)   She has to get them fully correct to get the mark

         (c)   They highlight areas that she needs to study

4.12

- Usman feels supported by the group and can ask questions when he is stuck.
- Usman can also read other people's questions and help answer them.

4.13

- Kit-Chi can pause the recording and reflect on what has been said, linking it to what she knows.
- Kit-Chi can question what has been said and see if the answers come later in the podcast.

CHAPTER 5: INFORMATION GATHERING

5.1 (b) Locating, extracting and storing information

5.2

Source of information	Paper-based	Digital	People
Books	✔	✔	
Family			✔
Magazines	✔	✔	
Archives	✔	✔	
Manager			✔
Search engines		✔	
Visiting speaker			✔
Journals	✔	✔	
Webinar		✔	✔
Teacher			✔

5.3 (a) Computers
     (b) Books
     (c) Magazines
     (d) Archives
     (e) Library staff

5.4 (b) False

5.5 Triangulation

5.6 (b) The questions may need to be reviewed to make sure that they are fair questions

5.7 (b) False

5.8 (c) Have a folder for each AAT unit and a sub folder for each topic or section of the unit

5.9 (b) Have a folder for each unit and dividers for each topic

5.10 (a) Magazine title, author name, publication date, page number of article

5.11 (c) The link to the webpage and the date the data was posted to the website

5.12   (b)   The brand name of a series of books

5.13   (a)   A breach of copyright

5.14   (a)   True

CHAPTER 6: TAKING NOTES

6.1   (c)   Provides a resource to help with studying

6.2   (a)   When you make notes on what the teacher is saying
         (b)   When you make notes on what you are looking at in a book or on screen
         (c)   When you save Web pages or electronic slides to look at later

6.3   (b)   A word that comes before important information

6.4   (b)   You can then read and understand the main lesson points more easily

6.5   (a)   Reviewing and tidying up your initial notes
         (c)   A stage which helps you understand and remember the main points

6.6   (a)   True

6.7   (b)   Showing how concepts and facts to be learned link together

6.8   (a)   Showing the stages of a process which involves several steps

6.9   (a)   It helps you to focus on what information you need to find
         (b)   It is useful for comparisons like advantages and disadvantages
         (c)   The layout is organised, making it easy to see information

6.10   (a)   Using your notes to learn the knowledge parts of the syllabus
          (b)   Using your notes to help practise the skills parts of the syllabus

6.11   (a)   Embedding information
          (b)   Trigger words
          (c)   Key terms
          (d)   Structured notes
          (e)   Offloading
          (f)   Refining notes
          (g)   Flow diagrams
          (h)   Key words

CHAPTER 7: WRITING THE ACTION PLAN

7.1   (a)   Can be about anything you want

       (b)   Must be agreed with your tutor

       (c)   Can be presented any way that you want

7.2   (a)   Comparing prices for 4 different brands of shoe online and in-store

       (c)   Writing notes on three online shoe suppliers and three 'high street' shops

7.3   (a)   An ordered list of tasks that will help you to achieve your goal

7.4   Suggested order:

       1   Find out more about the theme park's background

       2   Write about the theme park's background

       3   Write about the visit and what Sonia thinks about the park

       4   Write about what the theme park is going to change in the future

       5   Write a conclusion for the report

       6   Crop photographs to use in the report

       7   Put photographs in the report to illustrate it and make it interesting

       8   Do a cover page for the report

7.5   (b)   A column for notes

       (c)   Two columns for dates

       (d)   A task column

       (e)   An action column

       (g)   A resources column

7.6   (a)   When she was planning her tasks:

              •   Identified how long she thought each task would take

              •   Use the time frame of the tasks to decide how many to do each week

              •   Build in catch-up time in case she falls behind

       (b)   When she found that she had plenty of spare time:

              •   Review the timing of her tasks to make them more accurate

              •   Review the task start dates and start to do some tasks early

       (c)   When she started to struggle and fall behind:

              •   Review her tasks to see if she needs to do all of them

              •   Review her tasks to see if any can be made simpler and shortened, and then redo her timetable

              •   Ask for feedback from her teacher

7.7   (c)   It uses up too much time

7.8   •   Precious spent 3 out of 8 weeks on the plan – too large a proportion of the time allowed. One week should have been enough, including the time to act on her tutor's feedback.

   •   If Precious did everything to that level of detail then she is likely to take too long to do each individual task and she would probably get behind schedule.

   •   Precious may have confused herself with the amount of detail.

   •   When Precious falls behind and has to review her plan, she is likely to take too long to do this if she does not work more quickly on this task.

7.9   (b)   Important tasks may be missed or not done properly

7.10   (a)   If they are not detailed enough then something will get missed

   (b)   If they are not clear enough then you may not know how much work to do or how many examples to find

   (d)   It is important that they have 'to do by' dates so that all the tasks are completed by the project end date

7.11   (c)   Create review dates where you look at and, if necessary, change your Action Plan

CHAPTER 8: SOLVING PROBLEMS AND USING FEEDBACK

8.1   (b)   Factual error

8.2   (b)   Review the topic to make sure that she fully understands it herself

8.3   (c)   Add the column up at least twice until you get the same answer twice

8.4   (a)   Review the remaining tasks and see which ones can be discarded

   (b)   Review the remaining tasks and see which ones can be reduced in scope

   (c)   Review the time allocated to the new list of tasks and see where the time allocated to each task could be reduced

8.5   (a)   Sort out the problem as quickly as possible

   (c)   Decide what you should do to try to prevent it from happening again

8.6   (b)   Ask for help from your teacher

   (c)   Adapt your Action Plan to get the project back on track

8.7   (b)   Informal

8.8   (a)   Positive feedback which encourages you to improve what you have already done

CHAPTER 9: PRESENTING YOUR SET PIECE

9.1 (c) Arrange a verbal discussion of the issues raised by the questionnaire

9.2 (b) Presentation to her class illustrated by projected slides

Note: Phoebe is trying to persuade a group of people. She is aiming to promote discussion and convince them that food with a high fat content is bad. In essence she is selling 'good diet' and a presentation with lots of pictures is a good way of conveying the information for discussion.

9.3 **(a)** *'doesn't happen so bad'*
'it's'
'treated, like, fairly'

(b) You may have split the sentence differently and used different phrases, but this is one suggestion:

'Sustainability is about managing the natural environment for the future which includes making sure that global warming is minimised. Sustainability is also about making sure that there is economic growth which will keep businesses stable. Finally, sustainability ensures that everyone in society is looked after and treated fairly.'

9.4 (a) It is easier for the reader to find information

9.5 1 (e) Purpose of the report
2 (f) Questions to be answered
3 (c) Background information
4 (g) New information
5 (b) Linking new information to background information
6 (d) Conclusions
7 (a) Recommendations

9.6 (b) Ask your Study Buddy to read it through and make any necessary changes

9.7 (a) The animation was distracting
(c) The animation caused the talk to go slowly

9.8 1 The last bullet point is very difficult to read as the text is placed over the top of the picture.
2 The text of the bullet points is too small for reading from a distance (eg the back of a room).
3 There is too much text in each bullet point – this means it is unclear and will be difficult for the audience to understand.

9.9 All options apply – (a) to (f).

9.10 All options apply – (a) to (f).

Index